Palgrave Studies in Economic History

Series Editor
Kent Deng, London School of Economics, London, UK

Palgrave Studies in Economic History is designed to illuminate and enrich our understanding of economies and economic phenomena of the past. The series covers a vast range of topics including financial history, labour history, development economics, commercialisation, urbanisation, industrialisation, modernisation, globalisation, and changes in world economic orders.

Constantine Michalopoulos

Greek Foreign Trade and Finance

The Mixed Blessings of Economic Dependence

palgrave
macmillan

Constantine Michalopoulos
Hellenic Foundation for European
and Foreign Policy (ELIAMEP)
Athens, Greece

ISSN 2662-6497 ISSN 2662-6500 (electronic)
Palgrave Studies in Economic History
ISBN 978-3-031-92103-2 ISBN 978-3-031-92104-9 (eBook)
https://doi.org/10.1007/978-3-031-92104-9

Cover image credit: Rawf8/Alamy Stock Photo

This Palgrave Macmillan imprint is published by the registered company Springer Nature Switzerland AG
The registered company address is: Gewerbestrasse 11, 6330 Cham, Switzerland

In memoriam of:

My mother Antigone, who taught me about the importance of Greek national independence, and my father Nicholas, who fought valiantly in two wars to preserve it.

Preface

When I started studying economics at Columbia University, in New York City, more than 60 years ago, I had planned to write a dissertation on the economy of Greece. I had the notion that I would write something that would be publishable as a book and that this would help me get a job in Greece when I finished my studies. Indeed, I had made some preliminary inquiries about publishing my dissertation "Trade and Development in Light of the Greek Experience" at the Center of Economic Research in Athens, in 1966. Nothing came of it, although I published a couple of articles outside Greece based on my work at the time.

Then, in 1967 the Junta came to power in Athens and I did not want to have anything to do with Greece or its government at the time. My career did focus on international trade, finance and economic development, but not on Greece. Instead, I taught at US universities and worked for USAID and the World Bank with a focus on what are now called the 'emerging economies' in Asia, Africa and Latin America with a short stint, in the 1990s, on the countries of the former Soviet Union.

After retiring from the World Bank in 2001, I started spending much more time in Greece and studying its economy. I was there for extended periods during the boom years of the early 2000s and the miserable years of the debt crisis. During this period I started to publish various articles about the Greek economy in the local press and for ELIAMEP (Hellenic Foundation for European and Foreign Policy), the think tank in Athens, with which I had become affiliated. After I finished a piece on the Greek economy's recovery last year, I realized that I had learned a lot about how the Greek economy worked recently and half a century ago, but knew very little about what happened in between. Living through the debt crisis, I also appreciated that Greece had faced similar debt problems in the nineteenth century, but knew almost nothing about the details. Thus, I decided to study the history of these periods and write it up in a book. This volume is the result. A very small part in one of the early chapters is the result of research I did for the unpublished Ph.D. dissertation sixty years ago. Another part towards the end is based on work I did recently. All of it is a story about a country with people who are fiercely independent, but who had little choice but to enjoy and suffer the mixed blessings of economic dependence for two hundred years.

Athens, Greece Constantine Michalopoulos

Acknowledgements

The Bank of Greece has developed a strong reputation for its data, research and analysis of the Greek economy since its establishment almost a century ago. I am very grateful to its officers and staff for the help they provided in producing this volume. In particular I wish to thank George Tavlas, Alternate Governor, for his advice on several chapters and providing me with references and documents as well as for introducing me to other Bank staff. I also wish to thank Melina Vasardani, Deputy Head of the World Economy Division in the Department of Economic Analysis and Research and Athina Rentify and Effrosiny Alevizopoulou, two economists in the Division, for developing an updated series of calculations of the net EU transfers to Greece to be published for the first time in this volume. I reserve my greatest thanks to Sophia Lazaretou, Senior Economist-Researcher, in the Department of Economic Analysis and Research for her help in all aspects of my research but especially in drafting the story of modern Greece's economic dependence during the first century of its existence. She also reviewed and offered valued commentary on the whole volume.

I would also like to thank ELIAMEP for permitting me to reproduce certain passages of my Policy Brief 189/2024 *The Greek Economy a Decade Later*. Loukas Tsoukalis, ELIAMEP's President of the Board offered useful counsel. Manos Matsaganis, Head of ELIAMEP's Greek and European Economy Program, reviewed and commented on the whole book and supplied me with valuable references. I thank them both for their support. I would also like to thank Andreas Tsivourakis, a recent graduate of the University of Athens, who did an excellent job in developing all the statistical work and tables for the volume. Without his inputs this book would have never been completed. Danny Leipziger, Professor of International Business and International Affairs at George Washington University, Clare Short, former Secretary of State for International Development in the United Kingdom and Eveline Herfkens, my partner in life and work, also reviewed and commented on this volume, as they have done for several others. I thank them all for their continued support and help. Finally, I am extremely grateful to Ellie Duncan, my editor at Palgrave. Her prompt response to all my questions and her wise advice made a big difference in the successful conclusion of this project; and to Supraja Yegnaraman, also of Palgrave, for helping convert a manuscript into a real book. All remaining errors are my responsibility.

Praise for *Greek Foreign Trade and Finance*

"This a remarkable tour de force, presenting by cogent argument and lucid writing the long history of Greece's economic growth. The volume synthesizes Michalopoulos' decades of experience in global development practice with the objective of identifying the key drivers of the economic triumphs and catastrophes that the country has faced over time. It also provides a captivating exploration of the opportunities and challenges confronting Greece's future economic growth. The book is highly recommended for its comprehensive and insightful analysis; it is a must-read."

—Sophia Lazaretou, *Senior Economist-Researcher, Bank of Greece*

"Michalopoulos has written a highly readable account of Greece's unequal economic relations with her lenders and trading partners over the last two hundred years. Mixing scholarly analysis with personal reminiscence, his new book will delight specialists and lay readers alike."

—Manos Matsaganis, *Professor of Public Finance, Polytechnic University of Milan*

"Michalopoulos has once again drawn upon his unique ability to analyse complex economic issues with clarity and precision. His foray into Greek indebtedness over centuries provides an illuminating and often fascinating look into Greek finances and combines his deep knowledge of the country with his extensive experience as an economic pundit. A tour de force that should engage a wide swath of readers."

—Danny Leipziger, *Professor of International Business, George Washington University; former Vice President for Poverty Reduction and Economic Management, World Bank*

"An extremely readable and clear review of the trade and financial relations of Greece with Europe. The comparison with the issues for developing countries is important."

—Clare Short, *former Secretary of State for International Development, United Kingdom*

Also by Constantine Michalopoulos

Migration Chronicles (Revised Edition, 2023)
Aid Trade and Development: The Future of Globalization (2nd Edition, 2022)
Ending Global Poverty: Four Women's Noble Conspiracy (2020)
Aid, Trade and Development: 50 Years of Globalization (1st Edition, 2017)
Emerging Powers in the WTO (2014)
Migration Chronicles (2008)
Developing Countries in the WTO (2001)
Trade in the New Independent States (with David C. Tarr, 1994)
Aid and Development (with Anne O. Krueger and Vernon W. Ruttan, 1989

Contents

About the Author

Constantine Michalopoulos has worked on and written about economic development for more than half a century. In 2019 he was appointed Senior Policy Adviser at ELIAMEP (Hellenic Foundation for European and Foreign Policy), a think tank in his native Athens. Between 2012 and 2019 he was Visiting Scholar and Adjunct Professor of Economics at the School of Advanced International Studies of Johns Hopkins University in Washington DC. From 1982 to 1997 and 1999 to 2001, Michalopoulos served as a senior World Bank official including as Director for Economic Policy and Coordination and Senior Economic Advisor for Europe and Central Asia. Prior to the World Bank he worked for the US Agency for International Development (1969–1982) finishing as its Chief Economist (1981–1982). He was also Special Advisor to the World Trade Organization (1997–1999) and taught economics at several US universities. Following his retirement from the World Bank he served as a development Advisor to governments and international organizations including the World Bank, IMF, UNCTAD, the EU Commission, GTZ and the UK DFID, on international trade, finance and development. He is the author of several books and over 100 articles and monographs on these subjects. Dr. Michalopoulos is a graduate of Athens College and holds a Ph.D. in economics from Columbia University in New York City. Now mostly retired, he splits his time between Lusby on the Chesapeake Bay and Rafina, on the coast east of Athens.

Acronyms

ANEL	National Patriotic Alliance (Ανεξαρτητοι Ελληνες)
CAP	Common Agricultural Policy
CBAM	Carbon Border Adjustment Mechanism
CMU	Capital Markets Union
DAC	Development Assistance Committee
DHMAR	Democratic Left (Δημοκρατικη Αριστερα)
Drs	Drachmas
EAGGF	European Agency Guarantee and Guidance Fund
EC	European Community
ECB	European Central Bank
ECU	European Currency Unit
EEC	European Economic Community
EFF	Emergency Funding Facility
EFSF	European Financial Stability Facility
EIB	European Investment Bank
EMS	European Monetary System
EMU	European Monetary Union
ESM	European Stability Mechanism
ETS	Emission Trading System
EU	European Union
FDI	Foreign Direct Investment
GDP	Gross Domestic Product
GFC	Gross Fixed Capital
IFAC	International Financial Audit Commission
IMF	International Monetary Fund
LMU	Latin Monetary Union

KKE	Greek Communist Party (Κομμουνιστικο Κομμα Ελλαδος)
MOU	Memorandum of Understanding
MP	Member of Parliament
NATO	North Atlantic Treaty Organization
ND	New Democracy (Νεα Δημοκρατια)
OECD	Organization for Economic Cooperation and Development
PASOK	Panhellenic Socialist Movement (Πανελληνιο Σοσιαλιστικο Κινημα)
PSI	Private Sector Involvement
RRF	Recovery and Resiliency Facility
SDR	Special Drawing Right
SME	Small and Medium Enterprises
SMP	Securities Market Program
SRF	Single Resolution Fund
SYRIZA	Coalition of Radical Left (Συνασπισμος Ριζοσπαστικης Αριστερας)
UK	United Kingdom
US	United States
USAID	United States Agency for International Development
VAT	Value Added Tax

List of Tables

CHAPTER 1

Introduction

The Greek struggle for independence was long, difficult and bloody. It started in March 1821 and lasted until June 1832 when the treaty of Constantinople pronounced the new independent kingdom of the Hellenes, with King Otto at its head.[1] It cost thousands of lives and resulted in the destruction of farms and livestock that formed the backbone of the poverty stricken new state. At the time of independence, the Greek state had essentially no industry and limited, if any, taxing capacity. Its per capita income of 164.6 drachmas (Lazaretou, 2014, pp. 168–169) was perhaps 10–20% of Great Britain's or France's and not likely to generate significant domestic savings and investment.

Even before the country was fully independent, its revolutionary leadership had obtained foreign loans through supporters of the Greek struggle in London. And, in 1832, as soon as the new state became politically independent, it contracted a loan of 60 million drachmas (Andreadis, 1904), that marked the formal beginning of its economic dependence.

This history of economic dependence can not be viewed in isolation from the overall political history of the fledgling state. The politically independent Greek state of 1832 contained a population of only about 700,000 Greeks living in poverty in an area of 47.5 thousand square kilometers (Lazaretou, 2014, pp. 168–169). The bulk of the Greek population remained under Ottoman rule. The foreign policy of the new state

C. Michalopoulos, *Greek Foreign Trade and Finance*, Palgrave Studies in Economic History, https://doi.org/10.1007/978-3-031-92104-9_1

for the next 100 years centered on the objective of expanding its territory to include all Greeks living under Ottoman rule. To achieve this objective it was necessary to get the continued political and economic support of the Great Powers, France, Great Britain and Russia, which were instrumental in helping Greece gain its independence in the first place.

Economic dependence on capital inflows from abroad for a poor country in the periphery is not itself a problem, in principle. Indeed, classical economic theory argues that private capital should move from capital rich developed economies where returns are low to capital scarce poor countries where returns are higher and whose very poverty does not permit them to generate savings needed for investment that leads to growth, and that as a result everybody would benefit. But it is well understood that this does not always happen and private capital may flow from poor countries to rich, either because poor countries suffer from weak regulatory judicial or other institutions or because there are increasing returns to scale in rich countries (Rogoff, 2025, note 16, p.321). The state can also play a role in this process: needed investment in infrastructure, where the returns are too low or the gestation period too long to attract private capital, may require the state to borrow from abroad to finance the needed capital. So much for the benefits.

The challenge is that the returns should be sufficient to repay the loan, and most important, that they can be translated into currency acceptable to the foreign creditor. In this matter, government policy is critical as is access to foreign markets for the country's exports. It is because these challenges are often difficult to meet that in modern periods developed countries have established economic assistance policies to countries in the periphery that involve capital and technology transfers on a grant basis or on concessionary terms.

Modern development theorists have also argued that because development requires the importation of capital and intermediate goods not produced domestically, a foreign exchange constraint can arise separately from a savings constraint on growth, when foreign exchange earnings from goods and services are not sufficient to meet the technologically determined import requirements (Adelman & Chenery, 1966).

Greece was not unique in becoming economically dependent soon after gaining political independence. Many countries in the economic periphery have suffered the same fate. More than a century later, overturning 'dependencia' forced on them by the developed world became the battling cry of developing countries in Latin America and others emerging from colonial rule (Prebisch, 1950).

Greece's economic dependence in the nineteenth and early twentieth centuries, however, was voluntary, in the sense that it was not forced upon it by previous colonial powers; indeed the Great Powers at the time were mostly supportive as Greece tried to expand its territory at the expense of the declining Ottoman Empire—except during the Crimean War in the 1850s. Similarly Greece's economic dependence on US aid after World War II and its entry into the European Union were sought by the Greek governments for political as well economic reasons. However, both during the nineteenth century and more recently, Greek economic policy was not adequate to meet the challenges entailed in foreign borrowing.

All of the early nineteenth-century loans to Greece were eventually defaulted. They were followed by another effort of economic dependence through Greece's participation in the Latin Monetary Union, further defaults and the ignominy of having an international commission control Greek finances for a decade between 1898 and 1909. The official debt defaults in the nineteenth century were followed by stabilization programs predicated on the implementation of stringent periods of severe economic contraction enforced by the creditors which resulted in economic losses far greater than the benefits from the original capital inflow.

Greece was not alone in nineteenth-century official debt defaults—or for that matter of poor developing country defaults in the twentieth century and at present. In the nineteenth century there were an estimated 38 sovereign debt defaults, the bulk of which occurred in Latin America, in countries gaining independence from colonial rule and at similar levels of poverty with Greece. However, colonial powers such as Spain, three times, and Portugal, twice, also experienced sovereign defaults during the same period (Reinhart et al., 2023, p. 11; journalistsresource.org, p. 9).

This volume details the history of Greece's dependence in trade and finance, and the many challenges and benefits this dependence entailed over the years. It argues that Greece had no reasonable options except to depend on trade and financial links to Europe's markets both in the nineteenth century and more recently. It explores history's lessons on the appropriate policies that would have permitted Greece to maximize the gains from this dependence for the growth of its economy and the welfare of its people.

Chapter 2 provides a quick summary of Greek economic history for the country's first hundred years. The emphasis in the earlier period is almost exclusively on finance. The later chapters address both trade and finance issues. Throughout, the economic analysis is placed in the context of political developments that helped shape economic policy.

Chapter 3 discusses developments in the period 1923–1962 focusing on an examination of foreign trade and finance and its impact on Greek growth during the period 1952–1962.

The main part of the volume is devoted to an analysis of Greece's economic relationship with the European Union. This relationship, which has elements of economic dependence in some ways similar and in others very different from that in the nineteenth century, covers a little over 60 years, from 1962 to the present. It can be divided into three periods, each roughly twenty years long: Chapter 4 discusses developments in the first period 1962–1980 including the beginning of the association with the then European Economic Community (EEC), the period of the Greek dictatorship, 1967–1974, and the arguments for membership in the EEC which was finally accomplished in 1981.The main focus during this period is on Greece's increased dependence on trade with its European partners.

Chapter 5 discusses the benefits and challenges of EEC membership during the second period, 1981–2000 and the run-up to Greece's adoption of the euro. In these two decades, Greece's dependence increased, since as a full member, it was able to obtain substantial grants from the Community budget—as well as, on two occasions, loans to deal with balance of payments crises.

Chapter 6 details developments in the third period, starting in 2001, the first decade of Greek membership in the European Monetary Union (EMU) and the events that led to the Greek debt crisis. It argues that the crisis was caused by lax Greek fiscal policies and a rapid expansion of private credit. However, efforts to address it initially failed, partly because of weaknesses in the design of the EMU and partly because Greece, its European partners and the international institutions, in particular, the International Monetary Fund (IMF) and the European Central Bank (ECB) failed to heed history's lessons of how to deal with debt crises.

Chapter 7 analyzes how the crisis was eventually resolved and how its resolution has had a significant impact on Greece's future efforts to achieve sustainable and equitable growth.

Chapter 8 discusses the aftermath of the crisis, Greece's emerging relationship with the EU, as well as measures needed to improve Greek government policy and the functioning of the European Monetary Union. The last chapter discusses the future of Greek economic dependence on the EU as well as the lessons of the Greek story for other countries of the periphery seeking economic integration with the EU, with each other or with other developed economies.

Note

1. Actually Greece's political autonomy was established by the 1829 treaty of Adrianople; its formal independence and territory were established in 1830 under the treaty of London, but until 1832 it was supposed to be an autonomous entity under the suzerainity of the Ottoman Empire.

References

Adelman, I., & Chenery, H. B. (1966, February). Foreign Aid and Economic Development: The Case of Greece. *Review of Economics and Statistics, XLVIII*, 1–19.

Andreadis, A. (1904). *History of the National Loans* (in Greek Ιστορια των Εθνικων Δανειων). Estia. Project Gutenberg's History of the National Loans Release [EBook #34095].

journalistsresource.org. Sovereign-Defaults-and-Debt-Restructurings.

Lazaretou, S. (2014). Greece: From 1833 to 1949. In *South-Eastern European Monetary and Economic Statistics from the Nineteenth Century to World War II*. Bank of Greece, Bulgarian National Bank, National Bank of Romania, Oesterreichische Nationalbank.

Prebisch, R. (1950). *The Economic Development of Latin America and Its Principal Problems*. UN ECLA.

Reinhart, C. M., et al. (2023). *Sovereign Debt: 200 Years of Creditor Losses*. 24th Annual Jacques Polak Research Conference, IMF.

Rogoff, K. (2025). *Our Dollar Your Problem*. Yale University Press.

CHAPTER 2

The First Century of the Modern Greek State

Early Years

The Greek struggle for independence started in 1821 with obvious needs of financing the fighting forces and no resources other than those the revolutionaries could capture from the Ottomans. Their efforts quickly attracted support in European capitals such as London and Paris. Philellenes, as supporters of the Greek cause were called, organized in London two loans to help the Greek revolutionaries for 472,000 and 1.1 million pounds sterling in 1824 and 1825, respectively. Lord Byron, a famous philellene, who later died in Greece, reportedly gave a loan of 4,000 pounds to help Greek representatives get to London and negotiate the first loan (Andreadis, 1904, p. 10).

The proceeds of the first loan were quickly used up to meet the current expenses of the various Greek fighting forces. Only about 232,000 pounds of the second loan and two small warships built in the UK and the US eventually arrived in Greece. Half of the loan ended in the coffers of

This chapter draws extensively on the work of S. Lazaretou, whose many writings about the period, cited in the References, are fundamental to understanding what happened to Greek monetary policy and finance during the nineteenth and early twentieth centuries.

C. Michalopoulos, *Greek Foreign Trade and Finance*, Palgrave Studies in Economic History, https://doi.org/10.1007/978-3-031-92104-9_2

the London bankers and other intermediaries (Andreadis, 1904, pp. 12–19). Some money was used to purchase canons which never arrived; some to pay foreign generals and admirals who also did not arrive (Lazaretou, 2005a, p. 333).

The provisional Greek authorities stopped servicing these loans in 1826. While efforts were made to reach a settlement with the bond holders in the period 1826–1829, they failed to result in an agreement, so that when the hostilities ended in 1829 and Greece achieved autonomy through the Treaty of Adrianople, the new entity started its existence, essentially in default to foreign bond holders.

The early years of autonomy were tumultuous resulting in 1831 in the murder of Kapodistrias, the governor of Greece appointed by the Greek National Assembly in 1828. The three European powers, France, Great Britain and Russia which had played an important military role in helping the Greek insurgents gain their independence, determined in 1832 through the Treaty of Constantinople that there shall be a new, totally independent Greek state, headed by a king, a young Bavarian prince, Otto, second son of King Ludwig of Bavaria. The Greek constitution gave Otto power as an absolute monarch and established the Greek Orthodox church as the official religion of the new state.

Greece, at independence was overwhelmingly agricultural, with no industry and only some income generated from shipping. It is difficult to estimate its per capita income in current values or compare it to income levels in the more advanced economies of Western Europe. According to one source, it was 164.6 drachmas (drs) at constant 1914 prices in 1832 (Lazaretou, 2014, pp. 168–169).[1] Another estimate suggests that in 1870 Greece's GDP was about 30% of the average of the UK, France, Germany and the US (Lazaretou, 2013, p. 14).

To support the new administration, in 1832, the three powers provided the new state a loan of 60 million drachmas at 5.5% for 36 years (Andreadis, 1904, p. 27). Thus, formal independence was explicitly linked to a certain degree of financial dependence to foreign creditors. According to one estimate of Greece's GDP at the time of 120 million drs (Lazaretou, 2014, pp. 168–169) the loan may have amounted to 50% of GDP. The proceeds of the loan were used in part to mint the drachma currency under the newly established bimetallic (gold/silver) currency system as well as to finance current budget expenditures without significant use for investment. About 12 million drs was used to pay the

Ottoman Empire for a small extension of the territory in the province of Fthiotis (Andreadis, 1904, p. 28).

Otto's government did not service the 1824–1825 loans but did service, at least partly, the 1832 loan until 1843. It is estimated that Greece repaid 33 million drachmas from the original loan (Andreadis, 1904 p. 29) although the government was running budget deficits and had continued difficulties in doing so. From time to time it would request France or Russia to make a particular amortization payment ('History', 1977, p. 126). Great Britain was most persistent seeking regular repayment. In 1843 there was a bloodless 'revolution' forcing Otto to grant a new constitution limiting the King's powers. At that time, the new Greek government stopped servicing the 1832 loan.

Over the next twenty years, Greece was torn by considerable political instability and foreign power interference: the British navy blockaded the main Greek port of Pireaus in 1850 in order to extract payment for damages allegedly suffered by its consul Don Pacifico, a classic example of 'gunboat diplomacy' commonly associated with actions of colonial powers in Africa, Asia and Latin America.

Relations with the Great Powers deteriorated during the Crimean war. Following Russia's attack against the Ottoman Empire in 1853, Greeks living in Thessaly and Epirus, just to the north of the then Greek-Ottoman border, revolted against Ottoman rule and were supported by King Otto and his government. This did not suit France and Great Britain whose military again occupied Pireaus and Athens. They stayed until the end of the Crimean War in 1857. But before they left they forced the Greek government to accept the establishment of an 'International Committee' to review the government finances and its capacity to repay the 60 million drachmas 1832 loan.

The Committee, composed of the Ambassadors of France, Great Britain and Russia, labored for two years and produced a report, published in April 1860, which concluded that: (a) the Greek economic administration was inadequate; (b) that various government entities did not regularly apply the economic legislation; (c) there was no transparency nor accountability of the government actions. The Committee recommended a number of reforms in public finance and administration and that the Greek government pay 900,000 French francs annually to service the 1832 loan (Andreadis, 1904, p. 31; 'History', 1977, p. 174). In July 1860, the Greek government agreed, in principle, to make such payments. However, it did so only for one year and the loan was not serviced regularly in the next few years.[2]

The Greek political situation became chaotic and finally in 1862, another bloodless coup deposed childless King Otto, resulting in the termination of the Bavarian dynasty. In 1863, the Greek National Assembly, at the customary recommendation of the Great Powers, invited Prince William of Denmark to ascend to the Greek throne under the name of George I. In a gesture of support, Great Britain ceded to Greece the Greek inhabited Ionian islands. Soon thereafter, in 1864, a settlement was formally reached on the 1832 debts, with the government agreeing to the annual payment of the 900,000 French francs. It used for this purpose one-third of the proceeds from the customs of the island of Syros, the main Greek port at the time (Alogoskoufis & Lazaretou, 2002, Chapter 4). No doubt the Great Powers wanted to give the new Greek dynasty a fresh start.

In the three decades, 1833–1863, the economy grew at around 2% per annum, with most of the growth occurring in the last decade. There was some economic transformation with agriculture declining from 85% of GDP to about 70%, the emergence of industry (6%) and an increase in the portion accounted by services (Alogoskoufis, 2021, p. 17). Starting a tradition that would last to today, merchandise trade was always in deficit, with the payments being financed with capital inflows from the Greek diaspora and earnings from the merchant marine. The main export item was currants, amounting to over 50% of exports in 1859 ('History', 1977, p. 182). Because of the defaults on the earlier loans, there was no access to the European capital markets.

The Latin Monetary Union

In the late 1840s and the 1850s, large discoveries of gold resulted in lowering its price relative to silver and thereby caused monetary instability in countries using a bimetallic standard involving both silver and gold coins. This was a period of rapid industrialization and increasing trade among countries in continental Europe. Monetary stability was critical to promoting trade. It was also a period when France was a leading economic power and the French franc the dominant currency in many countries.

In 1856, in the midst of the Crimean War, Michel Chevalier, a French economist, sent a letter to Efthymios Kehayas, later Greek Minister of Finance, recommending to the latter that Greece join France, Belgium and Piedmont in a monetary union for three reasons: (a) reduction in the scarcity of money as members could use the French franc for all transactions; (b) the fixed rate among the currencies involved would eliminate burdensome exchange rate fluctuations; and (c) membership would increase Greece's access to the French capital market (Kehayas, 1875, p. 12).

A decade later, in 1865, under French leadership, Belgium, Italy and Switzerland did establish a monetary union aimed at preserving a bimetallic system of gold and silver at a fixed parity, with the French franc used as the store of value. The agreement, labeled later the Latin Monetary Union (LMU) had an economic rationale, but some perceived it also as a vehicle used by the French government to expand the role of the French capital market and France's political influence in Europe (Brabaroux, 2022).

At the time Greece was facing a serious monetary problem: the abandonment of the bimetallic monetary system by Spain in the mid-1860s led to an extensive circulation of worn foreign coins within the Greek market that were directly convertible into precious metal. The Greek authorities felt compelled to adopt a monetary system that was accepted by the European states, which were her main trade partners. Greece thus agreed to become a member of the LMU by the Law of April 10, 1867, with its membership supposed to start on January 1, 1869. However, in 1868, hostilities with the Ottoman Empire over the island of Crete, forced the Greek government to abandon convertibility of the drachma, thus rendering its membership in the LMU de facto inactive until 1870. The Franco- Prussian war in 1870–1871 and delays in the minting of the new drachma, postponed the implementation of the new system in Greece until November 1872. And then it was shortlived.

The first Greek silver coins were actually delivered to Greece from the French Mint, as required by the Treaty of Greece's accession, only in 1873–1874. By that time the price of silver relative to gold had dropped sharply, leading to a vast amount of silver coins being imported into France and Belgium (including from Greece) to be converted into gold at the fixed LMU rate of 15.5:1. This forced the LMU countries to limit the issuance of silver coins and eventually, in 1878, to abandon bimetallism in favor of a gold standard (Lazaretou, 2005b).

Unlike the other LMU countries, Greece did not return to a gold standard at that time. Indeed, starting in 1877, Greek governments embarked on a period of large budget deficits, exchange rate instability and drachma inconvertibility that lasted until 1884. Still, during this period Greece was able to obtain additional loans. In 1879, one of these loans for 1.2 million pounds sterling, at an interest rate of 5%, was used to finally settle the 1824–1825 debt. As a guarantee for repayment of the new loan, it was agreed to use part of the proceeds from import tariffs for 33 years (Alogoskoufis & Lazaretou, 2002, Chapter 4).

The settlement of the 1824–1825 loans improved Greece's apparent creditworthiness leading to additional foreign borrowing. "From 1879 to 1890 Greece borrowed 790 million French francs and 1.2 million British pounds. This meant that in a span of a decade Greece managed to accumulate an external debt amounting to more than double its GDP. A lot of this inflow was facilitated by excess liquidity in foreign markets which facilitated easy and inexpensive financing for developing countries" (Lazaretou, 2013, pp. 23–24). Some loans were used to help with the reconstruction of the new territories of Thessaly and Epirus, added to the Greek state as a result of the Russia-Ottoman war of 1878–1879 and the Congress of Berlin (see Table 2.1). Others were used to finance large investment projects such as railroads and building of the Corinth canal, with long gestation periods. The government ran a very tight budget in 1882 in order to prepare for a return to the gold standard. Additional loans were obtained in order to bolster gold reserves in anticipation of returning to the gold standard, which was finally done in 1884. The efforts to establish the gold standard resulted in a large overvaluation of the drachma with adverse effects both on trade and the economy (Alogoskoufis, 2021, p. 22).

Convertibility was again shortlived, lasting only nine months, until August 1885, because of the large domestic conversion of paper money into gold-resulting in the loss of 48% of the National Bank's reserves. In the meantime, in 1885 the extensive foreign borrowing had resulted in interest payments absorbing almost 50% of the government budget (Alogoskoufis & Lazaretou, Chapter 4). The drachma inconvertibility lasted until 1910. All this time, Greece remained formally a member of the LMU, but in practice, its membership had little meaning. Actual bimetallism lasted only a very short time and as a result had very limited effect on the real economy; if anything, the effort to return to the LMU in 1885 may have had an adverse impact on economic growth.

Table 2.1 Greece's conflicts and wars with the Ottoman Empire 1821–1923

Year	*Conflict*	*Result*	*Area 000 km^2*	*Population (million)*	*GDP per capita*[1]
1821–1829	Revolution	Independent Greek State- Treaty of Constantinople 1832	47.5	0.72*	164.6*
1854	Crimean War Revolt in Thessaly	Revolt suppressed - Occupation by Great Powers, 1854–1857	47.5	1.04	204.5
1866–1869	Revolt in Crete	Revolt suppressed	49.8	1.41**	210.0**
1878–1879	Russo-Ottoman War	Ottoman Defeat - Accession of Thessaly, part of Epirus, Congress of Berlin 1881,	63.6	2.00	211.1
1897	Revolt in Crete Greek-Ottoman war	Greek defeat - Crete Autonomous	63.6	2.45	214.7
1912–1913	Balkan Wars	Ottoman Defeat- Accession of Macedonia, Epirus, Crete, Aegean Islands, Treaty of London 1913	120.0	4.82	269.8**
1917–1918	World War I	Accession of Thrace, Treaty of Neuilly 1919 (from Bulgaria)	128.7	5.02	260.0**
1921–1922	War against Turkey	Greek Defeat, population exchange, Treaty of Lausanne 1923	128.7	5.94	265.0**

*1833; **two- or three-year average

1 in LMU drachmas at constant 1914 prices; *Source* Lazaretou (2014, pp. 168–169)

The International Financial Audit Commission

The period between 1886 and 1897 was characterized by large budget deficits, inflation and depreciation of the drachma. The Greek government was unable to meet its international obligations and after a series of failed negotiations with the external creditors, Tricoupis, the Greek prime minister, announced to the Greek parliament on December 1, 1893, that: "While the Greek government has the capacity to address the expenditures of its budget, it can do so in paper money, while payments to its creditors have to be done in species, which it does not have."[3] The announcement was accompanied with a unilateral suspension of amortization payments on the external debt and a 30% reduction in the payments of interest.

These actions caused turmoil among Greece's creditors and led to protracted negotiations, which went no-where for several years. In 1897, Greece engaged in another war with the Ottoman Empire which it lost and was forced to pay a large indemnity in gold coins. Greece was unable to do so and had to seek the assistance of its foreign creditors once again.

After another set of negotiations the new agreement provided Greece with a new loan of 150 million gold French francs to help it pay the indemnity to the Ottoman Empire but at the cost of having to give up its fiscal and monetary independence. An International Financial Audit Commission (IFAC) was established which had responsibility both for monetary policy and for oversight of the Greek budget and its allocation of different expenditures, in particular repayments of the debt to its creditors. With respect to the latter, the Greek government was forced to repay annually a fixed amount of 15 million drachmas (Lazaretou, 2013).

IFAC established and pursued for more than a decade disinflationary monetary and budget policies. As a result of these policies involving, for example an average reduction of 0.13% per year of the money in circulation, confidence in the drachma was reestablished leading to its large appreciation and massive inflows of gold but at the cost of much greater economic stagnation and adverse impacts on Greek exports than was appropriate (Lazaretou, 2013, pp. 48–49). Between 1899 and 1902 per capita GDP declined by 15% (Alogoskoufis, 2021, p. 30). Perhaps the most dramatic adverse repercussion of IFAC's restrictive policies was the mass exodus of the Greek population: Over the 1900–1910 decade 8% of the population emigrated, many to the US.[4] Over the whole first hundred years of its existence, Greece's per capita income growth was small, perhaps 1% per annum.[5]

The creditors also benefited: the progressive appreciation of the drachma combined with the debt repayment fixed in drachmas meant that they were getting more returns on their debt in real terms. These were further augmented by a treaty provision involving the debt settlement which required Greece to increase by 30% its repayments of interest and amortization when the drachma appreciated relative to the franc.

The unfortunate effects of the 1898 debt settlement led to significant political strife: Tricoupis, the prime Minister who signed the accords, was forced to leave the country. Deliyannis, his political opponent was assassinated.

More than a century later, huge crowds demonstrated in Athens against the undue influence that the Troika of the IMF, the EU and the European Central Bank were having over Greek economic policy in connection with the bailout in 2012 (see Chapter 7). For a time, the political parties that signed the most recent accords went into decline. But they quickly rebounded.

In 1909 the drachma reached a 1:1 valuation with the gold French Franc and Greece returned to the gold standard in March 1910; and to full membership of the LMU—although it appears that IFAC was still around in 1910 making recommendations on the permissible rate of expansion of the money supply.[6]

More Wars: 1912–1922

Greece continued to adhere to the gold standard, despite extensive successful wars in 1912–1913 against the Ottoman Empire and Bulgaria which resulted in a huge expansion of its territory, as the country's macroeconomic policies supported its creditworthiness and indeed resulted in increased inflows of gold.

At the onset of World War I, controls were imposed on foreign exchange as well as on gold flows. Gold and foreign exchange convertibility were suspended resulting in the de facto abandonment of the gold standard, as was the case for all the combatants. Greece maintained neutrality for the first few years of the war because of the links between the Greek King's family with the family of Germany's Kaiser. The Entente powers invaded Greece in 1917 and forced a change of government and entry of Greece on their side.

The end of World War I did not end war for Greece. Under the 1920 Treaty of Sevres, Greece was given, *inter alia* the administration of a large area around the city of Smyrna in what is now western Turkiye. When, in 1921, Greek-armed forces advanced into central Asia Minor, originally with the hesitant support of Great Britain and France, they faced opposition from the new Turkish government headed by Kemal Attaturk. Abandoned by the Great Powers, the conflict resulted in a Greek defeat, and a massive exchange of population, involving 1.2 million Greeks and 400,000 Ottoman Turks under the Treaty of Lsuanne in 1923.[7] The huge influx of refugees resulted in huge demands on the Greek budget and, in the absence of external financing, large inflation and a large depreciation of the Greek drachma, all of which will be the subject of the next chapter.

Some Preliminary Conclusions

The economic history of Greece in the nineteenth and early twentieth centuries—roughly 100 years from the start of the revolution in 1821 to the Treaty of Lausanne in 1923—was characterized by political turmoil, structural deficiencies in public and fiscal administration, frequent bouts of inflation and a poor record in servicing external debt resulting in bankruptcies and, on one occasion, external involvement in setting fiscal and monetary policy. Throughout, Greece was dependent both politically and financially on the three Great Powers, France, Great Britain and Russia that helped launch its independence and whose help was sought and obtained in the pursuit of national objectives. These objectives were largely achieved, with Greece's territory and population expanding several times over the first century of its existence. In the aftermath of the disastrous end of the 1922 campaign, there was considerable animosity against the Great Powers who initially encouraged the Greek incursion into the Ottoman Empire but later abandoned it. Still, the effort of liberating Greeks from the Ottoman Empire involved great sacrifices in lives and costs for Greece but, with the support of the Great Powers, was largely successful.[8]

The story on Greece's economic dependence is more complex. With respect to Greece's membership in the LMU, some have been very critical: "It is hard to see why the admission of Greece to the Monetary Union should have been desired or allowed. In no sense was she a desirable member struggling with burden of debt her nominal admission was secured on political influence...Certainly it would be hard to understand on what other grounds her membership was attained" (Parker Willis, 2018; Tavlas, 2019, p. 28).

On the other hand, as noted earlier, there were legitimate economic reasons for Greece's efforts to participate in the LMU, notwithstanding the fact that, as a result of wars and other external developments—beyond Greece's control—as well a certain amount of mismanagement, its participation was more nominal than real.

Moreover, as others have noted, not only with respect to Greece but regarding the functioning of the LMU in general, "The initial rules of the LMU were insufficient and incomplete...Rules can be changed and monetary unions can be resilient, but difficulties persist between countries with different levels of economic and financial strength... It is important to be able to tighten rules when the monetary situation changes and fiscal imbalances grow. But excessive austerity can constrain growth and increase poverty...Expansionary policies are needed in surplus countries to share the costs of readjustment between and not force all the adjustment on unemployment and wages" (Einaudi, 2018, pp. 19–20).

Poorer countries in the economic periphery such as Greece were able to obtain access to capital markets of developed economies usually on condition that they would maintain prudent economic and monetary policies. Foreign dependence was thus linked to the promotion of domestic economic stability. This is not in principle significantly different from the IMF conditioning its assistance on prudent macroeconomic policy. The Greek experience with repeated bouts of large domestic disequilibria and multiple debt defaults suggests that dependence on commitments to foreign lenders and fear of default is not a useful instrument for the design of effective domestic policy.

A significant number of Greece's public sector deficits, bouts of inflation and insolvencies were the result of the repeated wars and armed conflicts in which Greece engaged throughout the first hundred years of its existence against the Ottoman Empire (see Table 2.1). Public finances are extremely strained by large defense expenditures connected to wars or other armed conflict. But Greece's dependence on foreign borrowing and its contracting huge debts, which it was unable to service, also occurred outside war periods and resulted in defaults that were followed by periods of extreme austerity that damaged the economy far more than the benefits derived from the original loans. It is unclear how much of this austerity was justified and how much resulted from excessive demands of its foreign creditors.

The severity of the adjustment demanded of countries in default, the rules of operation and the relative balance in the adjustment of surplus and creditor countries in a monetary union are themes to which we will return later in this volume, as we discuss the second hundred years of the Greek state.

Notes

1. Using this estimate of per capita GDP in Drachmas it is possible to compare it to France's per capita GDP in 1832 of 2091 francs (Clio). If the 1832 exchange rate of the franc was equal to 1.1 Greek Drachmas (old) (Andreadis, 1904, p. 28), then Greece's GDP per capita would have been about 10% that of France.
2. Dallara (2024, p. 346) says that Greece continued to service the loan later on without paying interest but completing the amortization payments in 1973! Lazaretou (Lazaretou, 2025) notes that following the 1864 settlement, Greece was paying off the loan regularly until the further declaration of bancruptcy and settlement in 1898. Following another bankrupcy in 1932, the settlement of all the old loans was made in the early 1980s.
3. Translated from the Greek from Markezinis (1966, pp. 252–253). Opposition newspapers at the time stated that he said "Unfortunately we are bankrupt" in Greek 'επτωχευσαμεν.' Whether he formally said this is not certain; but the actions partially suspending debt payments occurred.
4. Including the author's paternal grandfather.
5. Alogoskoufis (2021, p. 10) estimates it around 1% per annum, but the estimate is not statistically significant.
6. The Commission continued to have an influence of Greek economic policy until the late 1930s. It was disbanded by mutual agreement in 1978 (Lazaretou, 2025).
7. Religion rather than language determined the population exchange: thus, it was Moslems that moved from Greece to Turkiye and Greek Orthodox Christians that moved the other way.
8. Following the Treaty of Lausanne, the only areas outside Greece containing significant majorities of populations considering themselves 'Greek' were the Dodecanese Islands, which acceded to Greece from Italy following World War II, and Cyprus, ceded from the Ottoman Empire to Great Britain under the Congress of Berlin, which continued to create conflict between Greece and Turkiye even after its independence in 1960.

References

Alogoskoufis, G. (2021). *Historical Cycles of the Economy of Greece from 1821 to the Present* (Paper 158, LSE, Hellenic Observatory). LSE.

Alogoskoufis, G., & Lazaretou, S. (2002). *The Drachma: From the Phoenix to the Euro* (2nd ed.). Livanis, in Greek.

Andreadis, A. (1904). *History of the National Loans* (in Greek Ιστορια των Εθνικων Δανειων). Estia. Project Gutenberg's History of the National Loans Release [EBook #34095].

Brabaroux, N. (2022). The Latin Monetary Union Experience (1865–1926): French Views on Monetary Union and Lending of Last Resort in Retrospect. *Jahrbuch fur Wirtschaftsgesichte*, 2022-0015.

Clio-Infra. https://clio-infra.eu.countries. France

Dallara, C. H. (2024). *Euroshock*. Rodin Books.

Einaudi, L. (2018). *A Historical Perspective on the Euro: The Latin Monetary Union (1865–1926)* (IFO DICE Report 3/2018).

History of the Greek Nation, 1977, Vol. 13. Ekdotiki Athinon, in Greek.

Kehayas, E. (1875). *The New Monetary System* (in Greek *Το Νέο Νομισματικό Σύστημα*). National Bank edition, 1927.

Lazaretou, S. (2005a). Greek Monetary Economics in Retrospect: The Adventures of the Drachma. *Economic Notes, Review of Banking, Finance and Monetary Economics, 34*, 331–370.

Lazaretou, S. (2005b). The Drachma, Foreign Creditors and the International Monetary System: Tales of a Currency During the 19th and the Early 20th Centuries. *Explorations in Economic History, 42*, 202–236.

Lazaretou, S. (2013). *From Default to Recession: The International Financial Audit of 1898 in Greece*. Gutenberg, in Greek.

Lazaretou, S. (2014). Greece: From 1833 to 1949. In *South-Eastern European Monetary and Economic Statistics from the Nineteenth Century to World War II*. Bank of Greece, Bulgarian National Bank, National Bank of Romania, Oesterreichische Nationalbank.

Lazaretou, S. (2025). *Note*. email 1/9/2025.

Markezinis, S. (1966). *Political History of Modern Greece, Vol. 2, 1863–1909*. Papyros, in Greek.

Parker Willis, H. (2018). *A History of the Latin Monetary Union*. Girvin Press.

Tavlas, G. (2019). *The Theory of Monetary Integration in the Aftermath of the Greek Financial Crisis*. The seventh Lectio Minghetti. IBL Libri.

CHAPTER 3

Greek Growth 1923–1962

Introduction

Greek economic development in the roughly 40 years between the Treaty of Lausanne in 1923 and Greece's association with the European Community (EC) in 1962 can be broken down into several distinct sub-periods. The first sub-period is between 1923 and the start of World War II. During these years, Greece's foreign economic policy moved away from the previous objective of 'Greater Greece' to economic development; albeit with great difficulties, because of the need for massive refugee resettlement occasioned by war with Turkiye and the great depression; and without much external assistance. The second sub-period is that of the War itself, 1940–1945. The third is between the end of the war and 1953. Following World War II, almost chaotic conditions prevailed in the Greek economy due to the destruction from the War and the subsequent civil war. The political situation, which did not allow postwar reconstruction to proceed smoothly, was probably the effective constraint on Greek economic growth until 1952. The last sub-period is between 1953 and 1962. It starts with the major economic reforms of 1952–1953 which set the stage for stabilization and significant growth the following decade and Greece's association agreement with the EC.

C. Michalopoulos, *Greek Foreign Trade and Finance*, Palgrave Studies in Economic History, https://doi.org/10.1007/978-3-031-92104-9_3

This chapter will briefly discuss developments between 1923 and 1952, but analyze in some detail economic conditions in Greece in the decade 1952–1962. The discussion will focus in particular on foreign trade and finance issues affecting growth prospects.

From the 1923 Treaty of Lausanne to the 1953 Reforms

The end of the 1922 war and the influx of a huge number of refugees resulted in several bouts of inflation and efforts at stabilization in the period 1923–1927. During this period, Greece was able to obtain a small number of loans aimed at supporting its efforts to resettle the refugees. Finally, in 1927, following the recommendation of another Commission, this time organized by the League of Nations, a new, politically independent Central Bank of Greece was established; a new loan of 9 million pounds was obtained; and a strict monetary and fiscal policy was followed with the drachma linked to the sterling at a fixed rate. Greece adopted a gold exchange standard in May 1928 and stability returned, for a time (Bank of Greece, 2009, p. 32).

The years 1928 to 1932 were characterized by efforts to implement an ambitious investment program and integrate the refugees into the economy. However, soon after Greece joined the gold exchange standard, clouds of the impending crisis started to gather. "Still, the Greek Government ignored the perils of recession and embarked on an overzealous fiscal stance to convince worrying foreign investors about its determination to stay in the system" (Christodoulakis, 2012, p. 10). This was followed by a long series of mistaken decisions and miscalculations, as the international financial system was collapsing. The effort to sustain the value of the drachma led to its overvaluation, and a drastic drop in exports. Eventually Greece abandoned the gold exchange system, devalued the drachma and repudiated foreign obligations in April 1932.

Post default, the Bank of Greece offered to settle with foreign bond holders at 30% of the bond value. This was agreed by most of them by the end of 1932 (Christodoulakis, 2012, p. 14) and a formal settlement was reached in 1935; but there was no return to the private capital markets for 30plus years. Still, despite the economic and political instability over the 1920s and 1930s the economy managed a GDP growth of about 2% for the period as a whole (Alogoskoufis, 2021, p. 33). This was achieved without any foreign borrowing after the 1932 default.

There is little to say about the World War II period. There was a huge inflation, destitution, another economic disaster. According to Alogoskoufis (2021, p. 35), "Real GDP per capita fell about a third during the period, and in 1945 it was even lower than the levels of 1833."

The end of World War II, again did not mean peace for Greece. There was a civil war that lasted from 1947 to 1949 which caused economic disruption in the countryside. The civil war's after-effects lingered on to burden the Greek economy for some time. For example, after 1950, upward of 100,000 farmers who had been removed from their farms for safety reasons during the civil war, had to be resettled. The basic problems of war reconstruction and political strife compounded by government inefficiency again resulted in a rampant inflation and a huge balance of payments deficit.[1] Nevertheless by 1950, there was some recovery, fueled in part by substantial economic assistance provided by the US, first, in 1947, under the Truman Doctrine and later under the Marshall Plan.

The assistance amounts were large: Over the period 1947 to 1953, US foreign aid amounted to about 10% of Greek GDP and more than 50% of investment (Iordanoglou, 2020, p. 23). This economic dependence was also politically motivated. It derived from the Greek government's desire and need for support to fend off the spread of Soviet Union supported communism in Eastern Europe and the Balkans. Unlike earlier Great Power support, it came in the form of grants or loans with a large grant element and therefore did not imperil the country's future creditworthiness.

In 1952, the Greek government recognized that US aid would decline significantly, a factor that undoubtedly played a role in stimulating a series of important monetary and fiscal reforms. The reforms contributed to the return of comparative stability and affected the future domestic and external evolution of the economy. The US aid reduction was a serious matter because the aid had been helpful in balancing the budget and in cushioning the inflation induced balance of payments deficits. In pursuit of restrictive monetary policies, the government forced commercial banks and the Central Bank to ration credit. The government also cut back its own expenditures on day-to-day operations and investment and imposed import taxes on a number of additional commodities (Gerakis & Ward, 1964).

The net effect of these government actions was to curtail the price advance and decrease imports. Though the measures prevented further price increases, the discrepancy between domestic and world prices at the prevailing exchange rate persisted. The time appeared ripe for a devaluation of the drachma. The devaluation came in April 1953. It reduced the dollar and gold value of the drachma by 50% and ushered a period of price stability and impressive gains in production.[2] Though there is no agreement on the immediate impact of the devaluation on production and incomes, there is little doubt that the devaluation and the reforms that preceded it laid the foundation for external and internal equilibrium later on and thereby stimulated investment and long run growth.[3]

The Growth and Structure of Output, 1952–1962[4]

Starting with 1952, the Greek economy generated an impressive growth of output. Between 1952 and 1962, Gross Domestic Product (GDP) at constant prices grew at an annual rate of 5.7%. Manufacturing production increased over the same period at an annual rate of 7.6%. While agricultural output rose by 4.4% a year, industrial output (manufacturing, plus mining, construction and power generation) rose at an annual rate of 8.7% (Table 3.1). Within manufacturing, the intermediate and capital goods sector grew much faster than the larger consumer goods sector. As a result, the relative contribution of the traditional light consumer goods industries in total manufacturing output declined considerably (Table 3.2).

The higher rate of growth for industry resulted in structural shifts in the composition of GDP by origin. However, the shifts were hardly dramatic: Agriculture's share dropped from 35.5% in 1953–1954 to 29.9% in 1961–1962, while that of industry increased from 23.2 to 28.3%.

Though the share of agriculture in GDP was declining, fluctuations in agricultural output, usually following a two-year cycle, appeared to dominate the year-to-year growth rate in GDP, partly because of the influence of agriculture on the food processing and textile industries, which used the products of the agricultural sector as their inputs. The two-year cycle in agriculture resulted in actual declines in farm output in 1954, 1958, 1960 and 1961. Industrial output, on the other hand rose consistently throughout the period.

If production is broken down by market destination, it becomes apparent that Greek output growth was evenly balanced between production for the home market and production for exports. Commodity exports grew from $115.0 million in 1952 to $242.6 million in 1962,

Table 3.1 Greek production 1952–1962

	Factor cost in million Drs. at constant 1954 prices		
Years	*Gross domestic product*	*Agricultural production*	*Manufacturing production*
1952	43,691	14,332	7,106
1953	49,902	18,071	8,284
1954	51,611	17,729	9,342
1955	55,453	19,304	10,092
1956	58,470	19,483	10,758
1957	63,452	22,499	11,421
1958	65,750	20,713	12,494
1959	68,600	21,818	13,832
1960	70,628	20,464	13,862
1961	78,904	24,752	14,952
1962	80,733	23,062	15,863

Source Greece, Ministry of Coordination, *National Accounts of Greece*, No.9 1948–1959, pp. 72–73 and No.11 1958–1962, p. 57

Table 3.2 Share of agricultural commodity exports in total commodity exports 1953–1962

	3-year moving averages at current prices		
Year	*Percent share of tobacco*	*Percent share of 4 top Agr. exports by value in 1962**	*Percent share of of all Agr. exports*
1953	40.32	66.74	80.21
1954	40.37	68.23	81.69
1955	38.60	69.00	81.20
1956	39.69	70.27	81.31
1957	37.80	68.17	81.61
1958	37.55	68.21	82.06
1959	34.75	66.25	80.22
1960	34.92	66.50	77.52
1961	33.06	65.40	76.62
1962	35.22	67.12	77.93

*The four largest exports by value in 1962 were also the four largest exports of any kind in 1953 and in most of the years in between. The commodities involved, by HS designation and in order of magnitude in 1962: 24 tobacco, 52-cotton, 08 fresh fruit, 20 vegetables and fruits
Source Greece, National Statistical Service, *Statistical Yearbook of Greece*, Years 1954–1962/3

a growth rate of 6.6%, compared with a slightly smaller growth rate for GDP as a whole. However, over the same period, exports of services, including emigrant remittances, grew at an even more rapid rate, rising from $65.1 million in 1952 to $379.5 million in 1962, a pace of growth of 17.4% per year.

The composition of commodity exports remained almost unchanged over the decade under consideration (see Table 3.2). In 1953, the four top exports by value (tobacco, dried and fresh fruits and cotton) accounted for 66.7% of total exports. In 1962, the share of the same commodity exports had risen slightly to 67.1% of total exports.

The implication of these data is that most of the growth of exports was due to increases in traditional exports rather than the introduction of new commodity exports. These traditional exports were overwhelmingly agricultural commodities and other primary materials. Agricultural commodities made up a steady 80% of total exports over the decade.

Of the ten largest export groups by value in 1953–1955, only the chemicals group was a manufacturing commodity. In 1960–1962, one additional group of manufactures, textiles, broke into the list of the top ten Greek exports. For the period as a whole, only a very small (about ten percent) portion of manufacturing output was exported.

Manufacturing growth was 'domestic-demand-lead.' "The rapid growth in manufacturing production during this period was directed almost exclusively to and reflected primarily the pattern of domestic demand for its products" (Coutsoumaris, 1963, p. 103). On the other hand, the growth in agricultural production for export was faster than growth for the domestic market.

Between 1953 and 1962, agricultural production grew by 5.0 billion drachmas, or 20%, while agricultural exports grew by 2.1 billion drachmas, or 42%.

The substantial gains in both agricultural and industrial output outlined above were due, in large measure, to sharp increases in domestic investment. Gerakis and Ward (1964, pp. 141–142) have pointed to the ratio of gross fixed capital formation to national product as one of the primary factors in the achievement of a high rate of growth in Greece during this period. Total GFC in constant prices almost tripled within a decade. In 1952, GFC amounted to 14.3% of GDP; by 1962, it had reached 24% (Table 3.3).

Table 3.3 Gross fixed capital formation 1952–1962

Year	*In million Drs. at constant 1954 prices* *Gross fixed capital formation (GFC)**	*GFC as percent of GDP*
1952	6,235	14.3
1953	6,847	13.7
1954	7,701	14.9
1955	8,840	15.9
1956	10,188	17.4
1957	10,376	16.4
1958	13,708	20.8
1959	13,731	20.0
1960	15,766	22.3
1961	17,988	22.7
1962	19,473	24.0

*Excluding transfers of ships to the Greek flag
Source Greece, Ministry of Coordination, *National Accounts of Greece*, No.9 1948–1959, p. 77; No.12 1958–1962, p. 54

In absolute terms, investment increased in practically all sectors. The exceptions were only mining and public administration. Capital formation in agriculture quadrupled in one decade. In manufacturing it almost doubled from 1,305 million drachmas to 2,177 million drachmas and in transport and communications it rose from 589 million to 4,490 million drachmas in constant prices (Table 3.4).

In relative terms, the pattern of investment showed substantial changes over the decade. A rising proportion of investment went to the transport and communications sectors (27% in 1962), while private construction investment amounted to a large 26% of the total. Capital formation in manufacturing dropped from 14% of GFC in 1953 to 11% in 1962, while in agriculture it rose from 8 to 17% over the period.

The increase in investment is attributable to a number of factors: Improved terms upon which credit could be secured promoted capital formation in both industry and agriculture. These improved credit facilities resulted from: (a) the establishment of the Economic Development Financing Organization which provided industry with loans of ten years duration at 5 to 6.5% and financed export industries at rates as low as 4%; (b) the establishment of the Industrial Development Corporation as an investment company to participate in the share capital of new industrial

Table 3.4 Gross fixed capital formation by sector, selected years

	Million Drs. at constant 1954 prices					
Sectors	*1952*	*1954*	*1956*	*1958*	*1960*	*1962*
Agriculture, Fishing	655	653	709	1,983	2,730	2,576
Mining, Quarrying	199	95	148	218	86	106
Electricity, Gas, Water	634	919	733	1,392	1,230	1,545
Transport*	589	846	1,222	2,747	3,593	4,490
Dwellings	1,808	3,143	4,074	4,539	4,683	6,024
Public Administration	58	209	200	84	226	181
Manufacturing	1,305	830	1,166	1,886	1,456	2,177
Other	710	996	1,259	1,241	1,886	2,274
Total	6,235	7,701	10,188	13,708	15,766	19,473

*Excluding transfers of ships to Greek flag

Source Ministry of Coordination, *National Accounts of Greece*, No.9 1948–1959, p. 77; No.12 1958–1962, p. 54

units; (c) low cost loans from the Agricultural Bank (Galanis, 1962, pp 19–20).

Increased spending by the government augmented capital formation in infrastructure projects. Government expenditures on capital formation rose from 2,564 million drachmas in 1952 to 7,204 million in 1962.[5]

Private foreign investment also increased substantially in response to government legislation offering protection and guarantees. Last, and probably most important, monetary and price stability after 1953, and particularly after 1956, helped to improve the climate for private investment.

Parallel to the investment increase, there was also a substantial improvement in labor skills, reflected in rapid rises in labor productivity. The 5.1% annual growth in labor productivity during this period compares favorably with productivity gains in other developing economies at the time and suggests that improvements in the stock of human capital also contributed substantially to output growth.

Foreign Trade and Finance

Foreign capital inflows add both to foreign exchange availability and the stock of domestic savings. In the introduction to the volume, I noted that economic development theorists and practitioners have frequently argued that, as development requires the importation of capital and intermediate goods not produced domestically, a foreign exchange constraint can arise separately from a savings constraint on growth. This will occur when foreign exchange earnings from goods and services are not sufficient to meet the technologically determined import requirements. In such cases, the growth rate achievable is less than that potentially attained from available savings and investment. The analysis does not consider other factors, such as changes in labor productivity which in the longer term have an impact on output growth. However, it is useful in exploring issues and options policymakers face relative to external trade and finance.

A foreign exchange constraint can arise only when a country faces a particular set of circumstances in foreign trade and finance: (a) technology must be given; (b) the substitutability between inputs in production and consumption must be low; and (c) narrow limits exist in the expansion of foreign exchange receipts in the short run.

Only indirect information is available with respect to the similarity between the technology employed by Greece and that employed by the more advanced, industrial countries at the time. It appears that many of the new investments that occurred in the period under consideration utilized quite modern techniques embodied in imports of machinery and equipment. Capital goods imports formed an important and steady portion of total capital formation amounting to 23% of annual gross investment (Table 3.5). Moreover, as Table 3.5 shows, imported machinery accounted for a very large proportion of total GFC in manufacturing, especially in the later part of the period when imports accounted for over 90% of total capital formation involving machinery. This suggests that the technology used was borrowed from abroad and employed a factor mix shaped by factor productivity in the more industrially developed countries. Without doubt, there was little choice open to Greece as to the kind of techniques it should utilize in the expansion of its productive capacity. It is quite unlikely that Greece could have developed indigenous production methods utilizing more of the factors of production available locally—particularly unskilled labor. Moreover, an analysis of Greek capital goods imports found no net import substitution occurred in the decade examined. Instead, there was a negative substitution in the sense that the capital goods absorption was higher at the end of the period than in the beginning. Imports of capital goods increased both because of increases in domestic demand and, as a result, of negative import substitution (see Table 3.6).

Table 3.5 Gross fixed capital formation by sector and type of asset

	Million Drs. at constant 1954 prices								
	1953	*1954*	*1955*	*1956*	*1957*	*1958*	*1959*	*1960*	*1962*
GFC Manufactures	930	830	955	1166	1530	1886	1405	1456	2177
Machinery	832	754	875	1017	1319	1475	1143	988	1501
Imports	562	571	660	808	1069	1361	1033	901	1451
Domestic	270	183	215	177	250	114	110	87	50
Plant	98	76	80	143	211	411	262	468	676
GFC Agriculture	564	653	632	799	1308	1981	2234	2730	2576
Machinery Imports	49	141	207	217	303	435	168	225	157
GFC 'Other' Sectors	5553	6218	7253	8223	7535	9841	10,073	11,580	14,720
Machinery Imports	598	798	1098	1145	1232	1532	1822	2137	3064

Sources Greece, Ministry of Coordination, *Gross Capital Formation in Manufacturing* (Athens, 1964) for the breakdown of capital formation by asset type; Greece, Ministry of Coordination, *National Accounts of Greece*, No.9 1948–1959; No.12 1958–1962 for statistics on capital formation; Greece, National Statistical Service, *Statistical Yearbook of Greece*, Years 1954–1962/3 for statistics on imports

Table 3.6 Import substitution in capital goods

Million Drs. at constant 1954 prices		
	1953	*1962*
Gross Capital Goods Production (P_k)	2,728	7,502
Exports (X_k)	119	140
Imports (M_k)	1,210	4,773
$Q = P_k + M_k - X_k$	3,909	12,134
$m = M_k/Q$	0.309	0.393

Demand Effect $\Delta M = m_0 (Q_1 - Q_0) = 2{,}542$
Substitution Effect $\Delta M = Q_1 (m_1 - m_0) = 1{,}019$.
Sources For trade statistics: Greece, National Statistical Service, *Statistical Yearbook of Greece,* Years 1954–1962; for production Greece, Ministry of Coordination, *National Accounts of Greece,* No. 9 1948–1959, pp. 72–73; No. 12 1958–1962, p. 57. Gross industrial production in the capital goods industries has been derived by using estimates of value added by industry provided in Greece, National Statistical Service, *Annual Industrial Survey*, 1958–1961

One interesting conclusion from this analysis relates to the differences in the relative shares of capital goods imports in manufacturing and in agriculture and contrast them with the output performance of the two sectors. Agriculture, with a much larger share of annual capital formation, grew a great deal more slowly than manufacturing. At the same time, the absolute amounts and the share of imports of capital goods in manufacturing capital formation were much higher than in agriculture. One reason for the contrasting output and investment trends in the two sectors may be that capital formation in manufacturing, mainly in the form of imported capital goods, incorporates more technological knowhow and skills than capital formation in agriculture, which draws most of its inputs from domestic sources of supply.

Special care is required when examining whether Greek foreign exchange receipts were fixed in the short run, in view of the crucial role this condition plays in determining whether foreign exchange availability played a role in determining growth of incomes and output.

Exports and receipts from 'invisibles' were the two main sources of foreign exchange receipts in Greece during this period and later on as well. Exports grew vigorously between 1953 and 1958 and stagnated between 1959 and 1962 (Table 3.7). Invisible receipts (services including emigrants' remittances) grew steadily throughout the period. What is not clear is whether these receipts could have increased even further in the short run, if requirements for imported goods pressed against the limits of current foreign exchange availability.

The assertion that there are limits to the short run expansion of foreign exchange receipts—a necessary condition for a foreign exchange constraint to arise—implies that either the price elasticity of demand for Greece's exports was low and/or that world demand for Greek exports was sluggish, or that the domestic price elasticity of supply of exportables was low.

Available evidence suggests the price elasticity of demand for Greek exports was low. A study of the subject at the time showed that the price elasticity of demand for Greek exports to the United States ranged from 1.02 to 0.62. Moreover, the range of the elasticities for Greek exports was the lowest among the elasticities of exports of the 13 European countries, participating in the European Recovery Program (Devries, 1951, p. 411). On the other hand, there was obviously some substitutability between Greek and Turkish tobacco exports. At the same time, it appears that Greek exports (except tobacco) and invisibles appear to have an income elastic demand (Michalopoulos, 1966). This implies that in a given period, foreign exchange receipts may rise despite a low price elasticity of demand for these commodities. The only requirement is that incomes in the importing countries rise.

Table 3.7 Summary Greek balance of payments 1952–1962

	Millions of US dollars current prices								
	1952	*1953*	*1954*	*1956*	*1958*	*1959*	*1960*	*1961*	*1962*
Exports	115.0	134.0	161.0	209.6	242.8	212.5	208.6	234.5	242.6
Imports	–244.8	–228.1	–300.2	–414.8	–481.3	–465.1	–520.4	–585.1	–661.1
Services incl Remittances (net)	11.8	57.7	60.7	83.5	127.8	195.8	214.1	254.0	266.9
Balance (Current)	–118.0	–36.3	–78.5	–121.7	–110.7	–56.8	–97.7	–96.8	–151.6
Private Capital (net)	14.5	27.6	35.9	49.5	59.2	46.7	38.9	57.6	97.1
US Aid (incl. Reparations)	117.9	66.3	58.7	53.8	28.9	40.2	36.8	32.5	67.6
Loans (net)	–9.6	–5.4	–7.3	12.6	–3.2	22.7	21.6	44.0	19.4
Errors & Omissions	3.7	–2.0	2.7	2.2	2.8	–1.8	5.1	–12.5	–4.4
Changes in Reserves: increase shows as -	–8.6	–51.2	–11.5	3.6	23.0	–51.0	–4.7	–14.8	–28.1

Source Bank of Greece, *Monthly Statistical Bulletin*, Vol. XXI June 1956, p. 34; Vol. XXII June 1957, p. 36; Vol. XXIV June 1959, p. 42; Vol. XXIII March 1963, p. 64

The picture on the supply side was hardly as encouraging. There are indications that considerable limitations to foreign exchange availability existed because of problems in the supply of traditional exportables. It could be argued that the development effort in Greece at the time drew resources away from the production of traditional exports toward new activities which were not export oriented.

A method of examining whether the latter development occurred is to trace through time the share, by volume and commodity of Greek exports in total world exports. If this share had decreased, and there had been no change in relative prices, there would be a presumption that Greece's foreign exchange receipts suffered because of deficient export supply (Maizels, 1963, pp. 120–124).

An examination of certain important Greek exports shows this to have occurred, particularly after 1955–1956 (see Table 3.8). With respect to tobacco, perhaps part of the decline was due to the 1958 devaluation in Turkiye and the resulting loss to Greece of some European markets. However, this explanation does not hold for some of the other commodities, in which the Greek share of total world exports has declined, as for example dried fruit, vegetable oils and wines. Even in the case of fresh fruits, where the Greek share of the world market had been growing steadily, supply problems persist. It was reported, for example, that Greece had been unable to fill the fresh fruit export quota allocated to it by the European Economic Community (EEC) in Greece's association agreement (see Chapter 4).

Apart from the supply problems, the single most important reason for Greece's inability to expand its foreign exchange earnings is Greece's apparent inability to generate new exportable commodities.[6] The same few export commodities accounted for a major portion of total exports at the beginning of the decade and at the end.

These data suggest that Greece had been encountering difficulties either in the supply of new exportables or in breaking into markets with new exports particularly manufactures. Either factor would tend to limit the amount by which foreign exchange could increase in the short run to meet increased needs for capital goods imports.

The conclusion emerging from this examination of the limits to Greek foreign exchange availability must be that, though there were several problems, foreign exchange earnings both from exports and from invisibles increased over the decade. However, the crucial question is a different one: assuming that some increases in foreign exchange earnings were

Table 3.8 Growth of Greece's main exports as percent of world exports

By Volume 1955–1956 = 100

(1) SITC	*(2) Description*	*(3) 1948–1952 Average*	*(4) 1957–1958 Average*	*(5) 1959–1960 Average*	*(6) 1961–1962 Average*
051	Fresh Fruit	59.0	200.7	181.2	258.8
052	Dried Fruit	84.7	107.1	101.8	104.0
121	Tobacco	63.6	120.0	101.6	89.3
263	Cotton	28.0	103.5	95.1	140.5
412	Vegetable Oils	42.0	104.8	39.1	21.4

*Estimates in columns (3) to (6) were derived as follows: with the average of 1955–1956 as the base, volume trends were traced back to 1948 and forward to 1962 for Greek exports and world exports of these commodities by SITC designation. The estimates in columns (3) to (6) are the ratios of the Greek export series to the world trade series

Source FAO, *Trade Year Book* 1955, 1958–1964

possible, did they suffice to cover the increasing need for capital and intermediate goods imports?

A Foreign Exchange Constraint

A number of studies of the Greek economy during this period concluded that a foreign exchange constraint did matter for at least part of the period (Adelman & Chenery, 1966; Michalopoulos, 1966, 1968). My studies showed that a foreign exchange constraint limited Greek growth in the period 1952–1954 and 1955–1957 but was about equally limiting with savings in the period 1959–1962, as rapid increases in invisible earnings from services and especially emigrants' remittances increased foreign exchange availability.

These results partially contradict the findings of Adelman and Chenery (1966) regarding the nature of the constraints operative on Greek growth during a period (1951–1961) similar to the one examined here. One conclusion of that study is that the savings constraint was limiting in the years up to 1957 and that the import constraint was effective in the period 1957–1961.

There are conceptual differences between the constraint model used in my earlier studies and those in Adelman/Chenery.[7] These conceptual differences notwithstanding, it is quite clear that issues regarding improved foreign exchange availability relative to the needs for imported capital goods and domestic savings, were at the forefront of Greek policymakers thinking. "The tectonic fault of the trade deficit lay just underneath the surface and created an uncertainty that restricted the safe expansion of domestic demand" (Iordanoglou, 2020, p. 111).

During the decade, the economy, especially manufacturing, was heavily protected and there were controls on the access to foreign exchange for services. Over time, the Central Bank diminished restrictions in the access of foreign exchange, but such restrictions were still present, for example for travel, at the end of the period. Zolotas, the Central Bank governor through part of the decade and several years later, noted that there was an excess of savings in earlier years (Zolotas, 1965, p. 54), and much of private savings went to housing construction. The main concerns were how to diversify and expand exports and how to access the European capital markets in light of the declining US aid. Still, despite the concerns about foreign trade and finance, the decade was one of monetary stability and substantial overall GDP growth.

At the same time, the Greek government was quite aware of developments in Western Europe affecting their main export markets: The European Coal and Steel Community was established in 1951 and, in 1957, the Treaty of Rome launched the establishment of the European Economic Community (EEC) of the Six. At the time, there were strong political motivations for Greece to establish stronger ties with the EEC. However, Greece was far too underdeveloped to consider participating as a full member in EEC—a situation not that different than that prevailing a hundred years earlier with respect to the Latin Monetary Union, involving some of the same countries! However, this time, it was possible to connect to the EEC not as a full member, but on the basis of an 'Association' agreement. Such an agreement was sought and signed in July 1961 and then came into force on November 1, 1962. It launched the beginning of a new era in Greece economic and financial links with the rest of Europe whose development will be the subject of the rest of this volume.

Notes

1. For a discussion of conditions in Greece prior to 1953 the best English reference is Eliades (1965).
2. The devaluation made the drachma parity equal to 30,000 drs. to $1. Later in May 1953, the currency unit was redefined by dropping the last three zeroes and the parity of 30 drs. to $1 was arrived at.
3. For support of the view that devaluation lead to long run stability, see Gerakis and Ward (1964, pp. 129–132) and Zolotas (1965, pp. 126–128).
4. This and the following section are based on Michalopoulos (1966, Chapter 4).
5. The government's share of total GFC increased from 29.4% in 1953–1955 to 35.1% in 1960–1962. Greece, Ministry of Coordination, *National Accounts of Greece*, No.9 (1948–1959), p. 77; No.12 (1958–1962), p. 60.
6. Zolotas (1965, p. 138).
7. First, in my model an attempt was made to account for possibilities of import substitution in areas other than capital goods and intermediate inputs. In the Adelman/Chenery study, actual imports in all categories were used to define foreign exchange requirements (Adelman & Chenery, 1966, p. 8). Second, the concept of foreign exchange availability employed by Adelman/Chenery included receipts from government aid and private capital inflows. This concept differs from the one I used here for reasons outlined earlier, and probably accounts for most of the difference in findings. Foreign official transfers accounted for a large part of total foreign exchange receipts in the early part of the period considered but diminished steadily thereafter. Their exclusion from foreign exchange availability would tend to make an import constraint much more effective in the early part of the period than later on.

References

Adelman, I., & Chenery, H. B. (1966, February). Foreign Aid and Economic Development: The Case of Greece. *Review of Economics and Statistics, XLVIII*, 1–19.

Alogoskoufis, G. (2021). *Historical Cycles of the Economy of Modern Greece from 1821 to the Present* (Hellenic Observatory, LSE, Paper 158).

Bank of Greece, *Monthly Statistical Bulletin.*

Bank of Greece. (2009). *The 1929 Crisis* (in Greek, Η Κρισις του 1929). The Bank of Greece.

Christodoulakis, N. (2012). *Currency Crisis and Collapse in Interwar Greece: Predicament or Policy Failure* (Hellenic Observatory LSE, Paper 60).

Coutsoumaris, G. (1963). *The Morphology of Greek Industry.* Center of Economic Research.

Devries, G. A. (1951, April). Price Elasticities of Demand for Individual Commodities imported in the US. *IMF Staff Papers, I*, 411.

Eliades, E. A. (1965, September). Stabilization of the Greek Economy and the 1953 Devaluation of the Drachma. *IMF Staff Papers, IV*, 25–45.

FAO. *Trade Year Book* 1955, 1958–1964.

Galanis, G. (1962). *Prospects and Problems of the Greek Capital Market*. Bank of Greece.

Gerakis, E., & Ward, N. (1964, March). Economic Stabilization and Progress in Greece. *IMF Staff Papers*, XI.

Greece, Ministry of Coordination, *National Accounts of Greece.*

Greece, National Statistical Service, *Annual Industrial Survey.*

Greece, National Statistical Service, *Statistical Yearbook of Greece.*

Iordanoglou, C. (2020). *Η Ελληνικη Οικονομια μετα το 1950* Τομος. Α 1950–1973 (The Greek Economy After 1950, Vol. A 1950–1973). Bank of Greece.

Maizels, A. (1963). *Industrial Growth and World Trade.* Cambridge University Press.

Michalopoulos, C. (1966). *Trade and Development in Light of the Greek Experience* (Unpublished Ph.D. Dissertation). Columbia University.

Michalopoulos, C. (1968). Foreign Exchange Constraint and Development: The Case of Greece. In P. B. Kenen & R. Lawrence (Eds.), *The Open Economy: Essays on International Trade and Finance.* Columbia University Press.

Zolotas, X. (1965). *Monetary Equilibrium and Economic Development*. Princeton University Press.

CHAPTER 4

Association with the European Community: 1960–1980

Introduction

Developments in the relations between Greece and European Economic Community (EEC) during the two decades 1960–1980 had three phases: the first, from the date when the Association Agreement became effective, in November 1962, to the military coup in April 1967 that established a military dictatorship in Greece; the second, the relations during the 'Junta' period, 1967–1974; and the third, the period of the restoration of democracy 1974–1980.[1] This chapter discusses first, the content of the association agreement and the reaction of the EEC to the establishment of the dictatorship. Subsequent sections analyze economic policies and developments in the Greek economy during the 1960s and compares them to the policies and performance during the dictatorship as well as developments during the period of the restoration of democracy. The last section presents the arguments for full Community membership.

The Association Agreement

The Greek government's economic objectives for the association were twofold: first, to strengthen Greece's trade links to the European market of the Six, which by then absorbed a significant share (32.8%) of Greece's exports and to obtain financial transfers that would be of economic

C. Michalopoulos, *Greek Foreign Trade and Finance*, Palgrave Studies in Economic History, https://doi.org/10.1007/978-3-031-92104-9_4

benefit. In a way, it was shifting the dependence on assistance from the US to Europe.

The Agreement which came into force on November 1, 1962, had three main components: (a) the establishment of a customs union—mainly on manufacturing products; (b) the development of joint action programs in fields specified in the agreement, such as agricultural policy, the free movement of workers, transport, rules of competition, economic and fiscal policy, and the harmonization of Community and Greek policies therein; and (c) over time, making available to the Greek economy $125 million to facilitate the speedier development of the country (EC, 1961).

The agreement was asymmetrical in that it provided for duty-free entry into the EC[2] of nearly all Greek manufacturing exports, while Greece agreed to reduce its tariffs on a selected group of manufactures over a 12-year period and others over a 22-year period. Greece also adopted the Community's external tariffs for these products vis-à-vis third countries. Many of the policies affecting agriculture were to be decided over time but Greece got a few up-front benefits: for example, special protocols (No 15, and No. 16) provided for a 50% reduction of EC customs duties on manufactured tobacco and dried grapes (EC, 1961, pp. 48–49).

The agreement functioned in this manner until 1967 with Greece benefiting over this period from its trade provisions and from loans from the European Investment Bank (EIB) amounting to $69 million. Trade with the EC increased with exports rising from 40.4% of the total in 1960 to 49.0% in 1967 and imports from 33.3% to 44.5% in 1967 (Table 4.1). Output, still dependent heavily on the performance of the agricultural sector, also rose substantially, at about 7% per annum between 1962 and 1967.

Some of this came to a sudden stop in April 1967 when a military coup took over the Greek government and established a dictatorship. The Community reacted immediately to "freeze" the relationship: It decided to "limit the operation of the Association agreement to its current transactions." This limitation was to last "so long as democratic and parliamentary structures have not been reestablished in Greece." The current transactions under the Athens Agreement were mainly concerned with the system of customs duties and trade relations between the EEC and Greece. Among the matters held in suspense were negotiations concerning, *inter alia*, the harmonization of agricultural policies and the conclusion of a further finance protocol to take effect after 1967; and

Table 4.1 Greek Direction of trade 1960–1980

	In percent				
	1960	*1967*	*1972*	*1975*	*1980*
Imports					
European Union	33.3	44.5	47.3	42.5	39.7
Other OECD	32.4	30.7	31.8	28.3	24.1
Rest of World	34.3	24.8	20.9	29.2	36.2
Total	100.0	100.0	100.0	100.0	100.0
Exports					
European Union	40.4	49.0	49.8	47.6	53.4
Other OECD	25.6	23.3	13.0	10.2	16.2
Rest of World	33.0	27.7	37.2	42.2	30.4
Total	100.0	100.0	100.0	100.0	100.0

Note The UK and Denmark joined the EU in 1973, but this did not materially affect the EU share of total Greeks exports or imports. The same is true for the share of 'Other OECD,' which was not significantly affected by the inclusion of Japan after 1967
Source Greece Statistical Office, Statistical Yearbook

negotiations for the harmonization ·of economic policies were not even begun. The granting of loans by the European Investment Bank was also suspended and the authorization of a further $56 million was blocked (EC, 1975).

The Junta Period 1967–1974

At first glance, the performance of the Greek economy during the dictatorship years was not significantly different from that in the preceding period. Indeed, some include the period through 1973 as part of the 'golden period' of the Greek economy (Iordanoglou, p. 179). GDP growth stayed at around 7% per annum but there was significant deterioration in income distribution, with the Gini coefficient rising to 0.43 in 1974 (https://www.wider.unu.edu/database/world-income-inequality-database-wiid). The EEC share of Greek exports stayed about the same between 1967 and 1972 and that of imports rose slightly from 44.5% in 1967 to 47.3% in 1972 (Table 4.1).

The economic policies of the Junta had not been examined in detail until recently, when a major conference was organized for this purpose. The results of the conference suggest that though on the surface the

Junta's policies were not damaging, they concealed weaknesses that were detrimental to Greece's long-term growth and integration into the EC. "The Junta bestowed an economy of the brink of recession and hyper-inflation, with higher inequalities, without modern structures, without industrial policy and a problematic credit policy favoring friendly companies that collapsed a few years later. Simultaneously, the dictatorship had interrupted the country's path toward European membership and tied to the US economic choices at a time that these were being shaken by the oil crisis and the dollar's instability" (Christodoulakis, 2024, p. 8).

Indeed, for a while, the Junta rode on the success of previous policies. Later on, many of its policies had short-term populist objectives: farmers were given cheap credit to offset their non-participation in Europe's Common Agricultural Policy (CAP). There were widely publicized efforts to attract foreign investment which in the end failed to materialize, and the increase in manufacturing production was a bubble in the absence of new investments that would embody modern technology which would raise worker productivity (Christodoulakis, 2024, pp. 11, 14).

It is also clear that the Junta mismanaged macroeconomic and monetary and foreign exchange policy in the period 1971–1973. Perhaps because the Junta did not want to displease the US, on which it felt politically dependent, the government insisted on maintaining a constant relationship with the US dollar at a time when the latter was facing strong downward pressures. This led to high imported inflation that fed inflation expectations and made double digit inflation permanent for a long period (Lazaretou, 2024, pp. 222). Of course, at the end of the day, the Junta collapsed not because of its economic policies but over a misguided and very badly managed effort to achieve a union with Cyprus that was thwarted by Turkish intervention.

The Restoration of Democracy, 1974–1980

As happens often with dictatorships, they collapse suddenly and without previous warning. This happened also with the Greek Junta in August 1974, when its plans for essentially extending Greek sovereignty over Cyprus were stopped by a Turkish invasion of the island. The Junta leaders, lacking foreign support, especially from the US which at the very time was in the last throes of Nixon's demise, tried to cut their losses and run. They invited Karamanlis, former leader of the conservative party, residing at the time in Paris, to come and form a new transitionary government.[3] He responded immediately and was warmly welcomed.

The new Greek government also almost immediately sought the unfreezing of the EEC relationship in a letter on August 22, 1974, followed by a request on August 27, 1974, for an "exceptional financial aid" of $800 million. The Community agreed to unfreeze the relationship and unblocked the EIB loan. Subsequently, in June 1975, the Greek authorities send an official request to become a full member of the Community (EC, 1975).

The years following the restoration of democracy witnessed both political and economic disturbances. On the political front, the new conservative party ('New Democracy') headed again by Karamanlis won the first two elections in 1974 and in 1977 but the second one with diminished majority. There was a rising new party called PASOK, the Greek initials for 'Panhellenic Socialist Movement'—a socialist party led by Andreas Papandreou, son of the previous Prime Minister. Its economic agenda was populist and its foreign policy wanted to follow a 'third world' approach and did not want to appear too keen on strengthening the European link.[4] And, in general there was a broad concern about reducing income inequalities and breaking with the past.[5]

On the economic front, the strong growth evidenced in the previous decades slowed down in the aftermath of the 1973 oil crisis and the subsequent global stagflation. The situation became worse in 1979–1980 following the second oil crisis. Over the period 1974–1980 GDP growth amounted to only 3%.per annum. Trade with the EC continued to grow with the share of exports increasing to more than 50% total Greek exports (Table 4.1). Penetration in the main EEC markets was and continued to be small—less than 1% of EC imports came from Greece; but the share of imports from Greece increased in all the major markets of France, Germany Italy and the UK (Arghyrou, 2000, Table 1, p. 153). On the other hand the share of Greece's imports from the EC declined to before 1967 levels (Table 4.1). Inflation, which had been over 10% per year for the previous decade averaged about 20% the last two years. Wages and salaries grew faster than prices through most of the 1970s but fell behind inflation in 1979 and 1980. As a result, real incomes of wage and salary earners also fell at the end.

The Karamanlis government, wanting to demonstrate a break with the past and, in particular, Junta's policies of favoritism to private capital, proceeded with the nationalization of several big companies, including

Table 4.2 Greek Growth 1952–1980

	In % at constant prices 2015 $	
Years	*GDP Growth*	*GFC/GDP*
1952–1962	5.7	18.4
1962–1967	7.4	24.3
1967–1974	6.6	25.5
1974–1980	3.0	21.9

Sources World Bank, Bank of Greece

Olympic Airways, a shipbuilding company and the Commercial Bank. At the same time, the pattern of fiscal revenue generation was more characteristic of developing countries than of Greece's industrialized partners of the European Community. Seventy six percent of total government revenue came from indirect taxes compared to 24% of direct. Income taxes amounted to only 15% of total revenue. The overall effect tended to be somewhat regressive (Table 4.2).

The ratio of investment to GDP continued to be relatively high—over 21%. But its allocation among sectors reverted to traditional patterns: A rising share, amounting to one third of the total was in residential construction. In 1978 the share of GDP going to residential construction in Greece was highest in all OECD countries.

On the other hand, manufacturing investment was falling and amounted to less than half of that going for residential purposes. The lag of investment in manufacturing was reflected in a decline of productivity growth in that sector. From about 6% per year in 1970, it was around zero in 1980.

The external accounts continued their peculiarly Greek trends. Exports were growing, but imports were growing even faster. Equilibrium was maintained by continued strong performance in the service sector meaning tourism, remittances and shipping, as well as continued inflow of foreign private capital.

In sum, the performance in the 1970s was pretty good, given the traditional structural weaknesses of the Greek economy. But the last two years and going also into 1981, overall performance weakened significantly. To some extent, this was due to external factors: Greece like all oil importing countries was hit hard by the oil price increases. This fueled already existing inflationary expectations and contributed to a deterioration in the balance of payments. In order to maintain equilibrium in the balance of payments and curb inflation the government's monetary and fiscal policy was restrictive, so that as a result, real output did not grow. At the same time, the inflation rate did not decline significantly. Growth in wage rates was below rises in prices, which helped dampen inflation but at a significant social cost (Michalopoulos, 1981).

Still, the application for accession led to a long and complex set of negotiations. Partly, this was due to the complexity of the issues involved, in particular relative to agriculture. In part, it was because Greece was only the first in a line of countries with Association agreements with the EC and the deal for its entry as a full member would be setting a precedent for the rest.

At the time that these negotiations were taking place I was working as a senior official in US Agency for International Development (USAID) in Washington and not at all involved in US policy toward Greece. However, I strongly supported Greece's entry into the European Community, both because of the trade opportunities that the entry would provide, and the opportunities for the inflow of financial resources, which I thought would continue to be necessary for Greek growth. Thus, very near the end of the negotiations, I was pleased to accept an invitation by Theodore Couloumbis, a Greek professor at American University, to address a group of faculty and students on the topic of "Financial Issues Associated with the Entry of Greece into the European Community" whose text is reproduced in part below.

"There are two fundamental reasons why the negotiations preceding Greece's entry into the European Community were long, complex and difficult: The first reason that Greece's economy is less developed and more fragile than that of most current members of the Community. When integration is promoted through trade liberalization, there is a clear danger that the trade benefits would accrue disproportionately to the stronger trading partners. The weaker parties—in this case Greece—need to be assisted in their adjustment to the opening of trade and to permit them to strengthen their economy over time and be better able to compete as equals. The form of the assistance is financial—hence financial issues are central to Greece's entry in the Community.

The second reason for the difficulty is that Greece is only the first of a number of countries in the Mediterranean seeking entry to the Community—among the others are Spain, Portugal and Turkey. The kind of deal the Community struck with Greece could thus set an important precedent for subsequent negotiations with the other countries seeking entry.

In addition to the issue of direct financial assistance, Greece's entry raises a number of other financial issues which are less direct, but which nonetheless could be of considerable importance in terms of the future evolution of the Greek economy. These issues have to do first, with the policy of the Greek government with respect to exchange rate management as it relates to the European Monetary System (EMS); second, with the implications of Greece's entry on the availability of private foreign capital, both in the form of Eurocurrency lending and direct private investment; and third, the impact of Greek budgetary policy as well as broad aspects of macroeconomic management.

In 1978, the Greek balance of payments deteriorated somewhat, with the trade balance reaching a deficit of $4 billion. The current account balance was in deficit to the tune of about $1 billion. There was a long-term capital inflow of approximately $536 million, leaving a basic balance deficit of $500 million financed by short-term capital and a reserve draw-down. In recent years, Greece has been able to borrow extensively in the Eurocurrency market. In 1978, this borrowing was approximately $400 million. At the same time, foreign direct investment has stagnated in the last several years.

In my judgment, the EC entry in the short run is not likely to improve the trade account deficit to any significant degree. The key variable affecting the trade balance is Greek trade policy pertaining to exports and the ability of the Greek economy to maintain its competitiveness and break into new areas of manufactured exports. Greece has done remarkably well in this aspect in the last ten years, but the rate of expansion of manufactured exports in recent periods had slowed down. Unless it picks up significantly, the trade account problem will continue and may not get any better, as a result, of the entry into the European Community. Over the longer term and after the agreements on the agricultural exports are fully implemented, one could expect a positive effect from the entry into the EEC in that sector; but the fundamental factors affecting the trade balance will still be Greece's overall competitiveness and trade policy rather than the entry into the EEC" (Michalopoulos, 1979). Efforts to strengthen the 'heavy industry' based on imports of raw materials collapsed after the energy crisis resulting in many 'problem' enterprises later on.

The EC agreement did provide for financial transfers from the Community to Greece. The instrument for such transfers was the Community budget, and Greece had obtained a commitment from the EC to the effect that its benefits from the budget will exceed its contributions to the budget. In this manner, there would be a net transfer.

At the time, the amounts were not precisely known, but there were some estimates by the Community as late as April 1979 based on what would have happened had Greece been a member of the Community in 1979. The European Commission had estimated that in the first year of Greece's entry 1981, Greece will have a surplus of approximately $110 million, i.e. the payments it received from the EC would exceed its contributions by that amount. It was estimated that the surpluses in subsequent years would rise to $300–400 million and ultimately reach approximately $650 million after five years. These were not obligations by the Community but rather forecasts of the probable effects of planned measures, assuming that the structure of the Community's budget stayed the same. The major principle was that Greece would receive net transfers of resources during the transition period. However, these amounts, if realized, were substantial in terms of the projected balance of trade and current account deficits likely to occur during the coming years.

Agricultural spending accounted at the time for about 70% of the Community budget. Most of the spending went into so-called guarantees, which were paid primarily to exporters of agricultural commodities. Some funds were supposed to be spent to reduce production of commodities that require guarantees. However, very little funding had been extended for this purpose.

The agricultural expenditures of the Community budget had a tendency to benefit North European agricultural exporters much more than Mediterranean exporters of fruits and vegetables. Under the agreement, it was expected that a good part of the total financing obtained by Greece would come through the benefits obtained from the operations of the Agricultural Fund. Specifically, it was envisaged that Greece would receive contributions from the budget amounting approximately to $40 million in aid for cotton production, $13 million in similar aid for dried figs and raisins and about $23 million for olive oil in the first year of operation.

In addition to the agricultural operations, the other main funding for Greece was to be provided from the operations of the European Regional Development Fund. Its total funding for the period 1977–1980 was going to be about $800 million per year, and at the time, it was unclear how much Greece will obtain through this Fund.

There were also many less tangible but perhaps equally important indirect effects that the Community might have on the Greek economy through essentially financial mechanisms.

A key question was whether Greece would join the European Monetary System (EMS). The main features of the EMS were:

- Germany, Belgium, Luxemburg, the Netherlands and Denmark had been joined by France and Ireland in a group of countries maintaining fixed parities in their exchange rates with fluctuations limited to plus or minus 2.25%; Italy had been permitted fluctuations of plus or minus 6%. The UK had not joined the exchange rate mechanism but was going to participate in other aspects of the EMS, such as reserve pooling and the currency basket. As with earlier arrangements, exchange rates were not intended to be rigidly fixed, since the rate could be adjusted through consultations among members.
- The system was to center on the European Currency Unit (ECU) which would replace the old European Unit of Account, a weighted basket of EC currencies.
- Participants would pool 20% of their gold and dollar reserves in exchange for ECUs to form a credit fund which will provide around $33 billion in short- and medium-term support to all participants and unlimited credit for very short-term support to members of the exchange rate mechanism.

Greece, at the time had indicated an interest in joining the EMS although probably not until the end of the five year transition from associate to full member status in 1984.

The monetary situation within the EC had important implications for Greece's economic and political development as well as for its trade and financial relationships with other EC members and with third countries. If Greece were to join the EMS, the Greek Central Bank would be responsible for maintaining a fixed parity with other member countries by pegging the drachma to every other currency and the ECU. Such an arrangement could have seriously limited Greece's flexibility in using exchange rate policy to affect the balance of payments. One of the possible problems of the EMS was that it was not easy to make changes in the parity relationships of currencies of participating countries.

Over the longer term, there was little doubt that the currency of a country like Greece would tend to devalue relative to stronger currencies like the mark. If Greece's ability to devalue was curtailed by pressure to maintain parity with a currency like the mark, it could have unfortunate effects on Greek balance of payments and monetary policy. It might mean that Greece could maintain equilibrium in its balance of payments only through strong deflationary domestic policies. For all this reasons I had felt that that "it would be rather unwise in my view for Greece to contemplate participating in the EMS until considerably later" (Michalopoulos, 1979).

Greece had been dependent on euro-currency credits for significant amounts of balance of payments financing. The fundamental factor affecting access and terms on which such euro-currencies were made available was perceived creditworthiness of recipient countries. Greece's entry into the Common Market and the associated commitments by the Community countries to provide financial assistance through a variety of mechanisms would have tended to increase the creditworthiness of Greece in the eyes of the international banking community. In addition, the closer commercial ties that were likely to result from entry would have brought with them additional financial contacts and the opening up of further credits, especially of the short-term commercial kind. However, I felt that "Greece indeed needs to be careful that it does not overextend itself because of the perceived ease with which it could obtain financing on private markets and it does not fall into the trap of assuming an international debt burden that it is not able to manage" (Michalopoulos, 1979).

It could be argued that the most beneficial effects on economic development through integration do not come through the traditional trade creation mechanism. Rather, the benefits come from the much more difficult to quantify but nevertheless important dynamic effects that have to do with the rate of investment. Following economic integration, the rate of total investment in the European countries increased significantly, not so much because of the inflow of foreign investment, although that also occurred, but because entrepreneurs' expectations about profits were raised as a result of opening up of larger markets to which they have guaranteed access.

I felt at the time that, "raising total investment in Greece, in particular in the manufacturing sector, is one of the key problems that must be addressed and that entry into the common market can have important beneficial effects on the rate of investment." This could come about in a variety of ways: First, Greek entrepreneurs themselves might start investing more when they are assured of access to larger markets in Europe. Second, there may be considerable amounts of European direct investment in Greece resulting from Western European firms wanting to tap the relatively cheap, yet productive labor in Greece. Third, there may be an increase of investment from third countries typical of the "jump the tariff' motivation present in investment decisions of American firms in the early 1960s. It is for this reason that overall climate of investment in Greece is a very important issue which the Greek government needs to address at present" (Michalopoulos, 1979).

In sum, the entry of Greece into the Common Market was likely to be overall beneficial. It presented Greece both with a challenge and an opportunity. The opportunity was the opening up of markets and the stimulation of investment. The challenge derived from the fact that reduction of import barriers toward EC products would mean additional competition primarily for Greece's industry. "To this Greece must respond by measures designed to increase competitiveness. It is very important that the stronger members in an integration effort help the weaker ones if integration is to succeed. It appears that a reasonable bargain has been struck on this matter and some amount of assistance will come from the Community over the years. Whether it will be adequate must be reviewed from time to time. But this assistance must not be viewed as the sum total of the impact of the Community. Instead, Greece should view the entry as an opportunity to come closer to the other European countries both in terms of trade, finance and other links in order to use these links toward a more equitable and stable economic growth in the future" (Michalopoulos, 1979).

At the time, there were opposing voices, primarily concerned about the impact of accession on the manufacturing sector: On the one hand, there would be increased competition from imports which would adversely affect domestic production and second, membership would not bring any significant increase in exports because European countries had already liberalized imports from Greece as early as 1968, and the EC had also opened its market to imports from other countries competitive with Greece (Papantoniou, 1979).

The Greek parliament ratified the agreement of accession, on June 28, 1979. Formal entry of the agreement into force came on January 1, 1981

(EC, 1979). In retrospect, much of what I worried about in the speech to which I have referred above came to pass—not immediately but later on: The warning about not falling into a 'trap of assuming an international debt burden that Greece is not able to manage' was heeded for some time—until the participation in the euro provided even more access to credits in the 2000s culminating in the debt crisis a decade later.

In retrospect, it is quite clear that it was not only the weaknesses in the Greece's economy that would have made entry in the EMS unwise. It was also the very expansive policies of the PASOK government that resulted in the rapid depreciation of the drachma. We would never know what could have been possible had a more conservative fiscal policy been undertaken.

I was at the time concerned about a number of issues that ended up of importance in the longer term. First, it was quite clear that in order to stimulate growth, it was necessary to stimulate investment and raise productivity in the manufacturing sector but also in agriculture and some of the services. This stimulus was essential in maintaining international competitiveness as well as in increasing employment and incomes of wage earners. At the same time, I was concerned about the structure of interest rates for investment, which favored residential construction. As long as these interest rates were negative, as they were then, there was an obvious incentive for residential investment whose impact is to keep productivity growth down. It was at the time possible to borrow legally at interest rates of 15% and redeposit the proceeds of the loan at 20–22% and interest income was not taxable.

Another old story was the tax system. Apart from the essential need to reduce tax evasion, a more appropriate structure of taxation would also have been desirable in order to bring a larger share of the population into the tax net. This meant an increase in the share of direct as opposed to indirect taxes as well as the taxing of groups, especially professionals earning non-wage incomes or even farmers, who were effectively free from direct tax payments. Such measures were important both from the standpoint of social equity and from the standpoint of reducing the budget deficits.

Greece was also going to face continued challenges in the energy sector. The Greek economy was, and still is, heavily dependent on imported oil for its energy needs. Oil imports accounted for a quarter of total imports. There was a need to undertake an internal structural transformation that would result in slower growth of energy use.

In sum, I felt that in entering the Community, Greece was to face a number of challenges. However, I also felt that there were some important strengths: I saw at the time the main area of future strength to derive from an excellent human resource base:

- School enrollment in Greece was higher than in all other countries in the Mediterranean basin and some in Europe, e.g. Germany.
- Greek entrepreneurial abilities and drive were manifested in all areas of economic activity both in Greece and abroad. It was too bad that sometimes they were directed as much in avoiding government regulations and taxes, as in activities, which benefit the economy.
- There was an active international community of Greeks abroad, who, both with their capital and their technological knowhow, had made and would continue to make contributions to Greece's economy.

The optimism derived from the strength of the human factor and the fact that Greek economy was quite resilient—much more than it appeared at first sight. It had survived and grown despite political change, government shifts or new constitutions. The material standard of living of Greeks of all categories had risen spectacularly in the previous twenty years, to the point that Greece faced some of the same dilemmas and trade-offs between quality of life and more growth as other industrial societies.

In the short run, the economic malaise from which Greece suffered resulted from a combination of external shocks superimposed on a number of structural weaknesses. Moreover, an expansionary fiscal policy and an enlargement of the public sector was totally inappropriate in handling the external shocks and made it impossible to realign policies with those of the European partners The situation would not have improved without curtailing inflation. But the costs of belt tightening should have been borne more equitably.

In the longer term, there was a need to promote productivity growth and structural change in order to regain the growth rates achieved in the past. The problems were not insuperable. But it was necessary to develop a community of purpose and a sense that the benefits from growth will be equitably shared. An important step in that direction was much needed tax reform.

"If government policies do not result in equitable distribution of benefits and burdens, experience in many parts of the world suggests that growth itself may not be sustainable. At the same time, direct government intervention may not always be the solution. Rather it could lead to the establishment of rules and regulations that pose through their very creation a challenge for people to avoid with inefficiencies and inequities the only result. The balance between private initiative and public sector involvement in the promotion of growth with equity is a delicate.one. How well Greek society deals with this issue will have a significant bearing on how the Greek economy does in the 1980s" (Michalopoulos, 1981).

The Karamanlis government pushed very hard for entry into the European Community at least as much for political and foreign policy reasons as for economic ones. Karamanlis was convinced of the importance of Greece belonging to this group of Western European democracies as a counterbalance to Greece's relations with the US: these were at a low point because of Greece's abandoning NATO's military command in 1974 in the aftermath of the Cyprus debacle (Psalidopoulos, 2024). In the end, the government succeeded, in returning Greece to the NATO military command in the spring of 1980 and entering the EC on January 1, 1981.

Notes

1. In Greek, 'Μεταπολιτευση'.
2. The terms 'European Community' (EC) and European Economic Community (EEC) are used interchangeably.
3. Notwithstanding the fact that Karamanlis had in 1973 published a strong letter openly criticizing the noxious regime.
4. Its populist slogan which rhymed in Greek was "EEC and NATO, the same syndicate".
5. See also 'The Oxford Handbook on Modern Greek Politics' (edited by K. Featherstone, D. A. Sotiropoulos). Oxford: Oxford University Press.

References

Arghyrou, M. G. (2000). EU Participation and the External Trade of Greece: An Appraisal of the Evidence. *Applied Economics, 32*(2), 151–159.

Christodoulakis, N. (Ed.). (2024). Preface. In *The Economics of the Dictatorship, 1967–1974*. Greek Parliament.

EC. (1961). *Official Journal of the European Communities 293/63* "Council Decision of 23 September 1961" (63/106/EEC).

EC. (1975). *Commission of the European Communities, Information Directorate* (Information Note 105/75) "Greece and the European Community".

EC. (1979, November 19). *Official Journal of the European Communities*, L291, "Legislation", "Act Concerning the Conditions of Accession of the Hellenic Republic and the Adjustment of the Treaties".

Greece, Ministry of Coordination, *National Accounts of Greece.*

Greece, National Statistical Service, *Statistical Yearbook of Greece.*

Lazaretou, S. (2024). The Greek Experience During the Period of Great Inflation. In N. Chridtodoulakis (Ed.), *The Economics of the Dictatorship, 1967–1974.* Greek Parliament.

Michalopoulos, C. (1979, May 18). *Financial Issues Associated with the Entry of Greece into European Community.* Paper Presented at Seminar, American University, Washington DC.

Michalopoulos, C. (1981, April). *Prospects for the Greek Economy in the 1980's.* Paper Presented at the Atheneum Club, London.

Papantoniou, J. (1979). Foreign Trade and Industrial Development: Greece and the EU. *Cambridge Journal of Economics, 5*, 31–48.

Psalisdopoulos, M. (2024, September 29). Nationalizations, Extra Taxes and the Turn Toward the EU: Truths and Myths About Economic Policy After 1974 (in Greek 'Κρατικοποιησεις, εκτατοι φοροι, και στροφη προς την ΕΟΚ¨Αληθειες και μυθοι για την οιονομκη πολιτικη μετα το 1974'). *Kathimerini.*

CHAPTER 5

Greece in the European Community: 1981–2000

Introduction

Greece entered the European Community with considerable structural weaknesses and macroeconomic imbalances at a time that the world was just recovering from the 1979 oil shock. It had a much larger agricultural sector than the EU average, a manufacturing sector that had grown behind heavy protection and a budget deficit that was not large, but had been growing. It also had a Central Bank that was not independent in setting monetary policy and a tax system that permitted evasion for many self-employed. These were weaknesses that would be exacerbated by the increased competition resulting from entry into the European Community.

Greece's participation for the first twenty years of its membership can be divided into two periods: The first decade, roughly from 1981 to 1990, was driven by the populist agenda of the PASOK government which won the 1981 and 1985 elections. Its economic priorities, which were supported by a large share of the Greek populace, involved significant governmental efforts to develop a more equitable society through welfare programs, tax reforms and other measures including the nationalization of industry. But it also resulted in a mushrooming of government bureaucracy, large budget deficits, high inflation, balance of payments difficulties and stagnant economic growth.

C. Michalopoulos, *Greek Foreign Trade and Finance*, Palgrave Studies in Economic History, https://doi.org/10.1007/978-3-031-92104-9_5

The second period started roughly in 1990 with the win of the center right—New Democracy government in the Greek elections of that year and its decision to abide by the provisions of the new Maastricht Treaty which was agreed in the EU in 1992 and took effect in 1993. The early 1990s witnessed efforts to stabilize the economy and restore growth as well as eventually integrate Greece more into the European institutions, including the EMS. Later in the decade, the new PASOK governments, elected in 1993 and 1996 and especially the second one, headed by Simitis, were committed to take the very difficult steps that would permit Greece to meet the criteria needed to join the euro in 2001, two years after its launching.

The First Decade

The PASOK government, elected in October 1981, did so on a promise of 'change.' The change had three components: (a) wage policy, including wage increases of 48% to lower wage strata, and automatic wage indexation every four months to protect real wages and pensions; (b) taxation policy, which involved raising corporate and income tax rates, but did not affect the self-employed who continued to evade taxes; (c) a 'socialization' policy, which involved first, setting up a new agency that took over 48 loss making private enterprises whose losses became an albatross on public finances; and second, postponing a number of major infrastructure projects started by the previous government (Alogoskoufis, 2021, p. 47).

The increases in corporate taxes were not sufficient to offset the significant increases in government programs. The result was a large increase in budget deficits, an explosive rise in public debt and high inflation. Government deficits rose from an average of 2.6% in the period 1974–1980 to more than 10% in the 1980s reaching a high of 15.9% in 1990. As a result, public debt rose from 27% of GDP in 1980 to 89% in 1990 and inflation, from an average of around 10% in the late 1970s, to 20% for the decade of the 1980s (Iordanoglou, 2004). At the same time, unemployment rose from around 2% in the second half of the 1970s to 7.5% on average in the 1980s despite increases in public sector employment. The overall result was stagflation, with no overall increase in per capita income for the decade as a whole.

On the other hand, early on, in 1981–1982 the policies resulted in significant improvements in income distribution from the levels reached during the Junta years. After that, both income and consumption distribution indices stayed flat until 1994 and improved slightly in the period 1994–1999—but the latter was not statistically significant (Mitrakos & Tsakloglou, p. 34). Over the decade of the 1990s as a whole, the Gini coefficients for Greece were in the range of 0.33–0.35, slightly higher than the OECD median[1] (https://www.wider.unu.edu/database/world-income-inequality-database-wiid).

The macroeconomic policies of the PASOK government led to increased current account deficits (see Table 5.1) and pressure on the drachma, which, wisely, had not been connected to the ECU. A study comparing productivity in three recently acceding countries, Greece, Portugal and Spain found that in the case of Greece, total factor productivity for the decade of the 1980s was actually negative, compared to an annual growth of 0.7% in Portugal and 1.3% in Spain (Bryant et al., 2001, p. 13).

As part of the accession agreement Greece had agreed to eliminate by 1986: (a) import duties on EEC products; (b) a number of other discriminatory practices against imported products, including higher taxation, quantitative restrictions and partial up-front payment of invoices; (c) export subsidies. It appears that, except for a few very highly protected industries, the problems with import competition did not derive so much from the elimination of the import duties, which were relatively low, but from the reductions in the non-duty impediments to imports. At the same time, the competitiveness of Greek exports deteriorated in products such as textiles, vegetables and base metals in major European markets such as France and Germany (Arghyrou, 2000, p. 153).

In 1982 the Greek government sought and obtained an extension of the non-duty restraints on EEC imports through the imposition of an alternative 'additive' tax that was to be eliminated by 1989. In 1983 there was a 15.5% devaluation of the drachma. But the pressure continued.

In 1985 the PASOK government, which in its pre-election campaigns in the late 1970s had opposed EEC entry, found itself having to seek external assistance to deal with a severe balance of payments problem. It had two options: either obtain aid from the IMF or seek support from Brussels. It chose the latter, I suspect because going hat-in-hand to the IMF would have been politically unacceptable to its domestic constituency as the IMF would have been too closely identified with the US and 'Washington.'

Table 5.1 Greece—summary balance of payments

	Million US$ Current Prices and Percent							
Items	*1965*	*1970*	*1976*	*1980*	*1985*	*1990*	*1995*	*2000*
Imports-Goods	914	1509	4997	9717	9370	16,564	20,343	30,322
Exports-Goods	331	612	2258	4175	4357	6458	5918	10,120
Trade Balance	−583	−897	−2739	−5542	−5013	−10,106	−14,425	−20,201
Net Services	303	491	1131	2519	1199	3560	5237	7915
Current Account	−280	−406	−929	−2209	−3276	−3537	−2864	−9820
CA Balance/GDP	5.3%	4.7%	3.0%	3.9%	6.9%	3.6%	2.1%	7.6%

Source World Bank WDI

The government was able to obtain two kinds of relief: First, it was able to extend the imposition of export subsidies and second it was able to secure a 'medium term' loan of 1.75 billion ECU to be disbursed in two installments, one immediately and one in 1987 (EC, 1985).[2] The loan included the kind of conditionality usually found in IMF 'standbys' including quantitative commitments to reduce public sector borrowing, domestic credit expansion, the current account deficit and the rate of inflation.

Looking back at the performance of the Greek economy in the years following the loan, it is quite clear that while the government made some progress in reducing the deficit and inflation in 1986 and 1987, it clearly failed to meet several important quantitative targets set in the loan for these two years as well as the improvements in the current account deficit projected for 1988. The conditions were:

- A slow-down in inflation so that the annual rate of price increase is brought down to 15% at the end of 1986 and under 10% by mid-1987. The price index (consumer or producer) was not specified. The actual increase in the consumer price index was 23.0% for 1986 and 16.4% in 1987. The producer price index increased by 17.9% for 1986 and 9.7% for 1987 (Bank of Greece, 1987, p. 125).
- A non-quantitative target on reduction in the labor costs.
- A reduction in the public sector borrowing requirements by 4 percentage points in 1986 and 4 percentage points in 1987. This was achieved for 1986. But there was less than 1% reduction in 1987 (Bank of Greece, 1987, p. 67).
- A domestic credit reduction of 17% in 1986 and 10% in 1987.Both of these were achieved (Bank of Greece, 1987, p. 98).
- A reduction of the balance of payments on current account by 1988 so that there would be no increase in public debt. This was an inoperative condition as it pertained to the beginning of 1988—by which time the second tranche was disbursed—and in any case was not met.

On balance, several of the loan conditions were met. Others were not.[3] But enough progress was made for Brussels to disburse the second tranche (Bank of Greece, 1987, p. 171). After the improvements in the macroeconomic situation in 1986 and 1987, Papandreou fired his Minister of the Economy, K. Simitis and the fiscal imbalance deteriorated

Table 5.2 Greece—GDP Growth, GFC 1980–2000

	In percent and at 2015 constant prices		
Years	*GDP growth*	*GFC/GDP*	*EU Net/GDP*
1980–1990	0.7	17.6	2.0*
1990–2000	2.2	17.5	3.4

*1981–1990

Sources World Bank, Bank of Greece

again drastically in 1988–1990, reaching a deficit of 15.9% in the latter year (Table 5.2).

Throughout this period, the Association agreement resulted in Greece receiving progressively larger amounts of payments, first primarily from EEC's European Agricultural Guarantee and Guidance Fund (EAGGF) and later from the Regional Development Fund. The net payments (gross receipts—minus Greece's contributions to the EEC budget) started from a low 132.7 million ECUs in 1981 to 561.4 million ECUs in 1982, 1.139 million in 1985 and 2.362 million in 1989 (see Table 5.3). This involved increases from 1% of GDP in 1981–1982 to 2.5% in 1986 and almost 3% at the end of the decade. The amounts received were actually larger than those estimated in advance of Greece's entry discussed in Chapter 4.

An early analysis of the transfers showed that they accounted for a significant and rising proportion of both public investment outlays and government transfers to the agricultural sector. In the case of the former they rose from nothing to over 75% of public sector GFC in 2000. For agriculture, EU transfers were roughly two-thirds to three quarters of public sector supports from the very beginning of the accession (Spraos, 2001, p. 284). However, the overall investment rate as a fraction of GDP failed to return to the levels of achieved in the previous two decades. Foreign private direct investment also failed to increase and the nationalization of ailing enterprises imposed a lasting burden on the budget.

The net effect of Greece's accession to the EU even from the beginning was increased dependence on Europe for financial support. In a sense this achieved Greece's objective of shifting its dependence away from the US to Europe. In the second decade of its membership the average share of EC aid was 3.4% of Greek GDP compared to 4.0% of US aid annually for

Table 5.3 EU net contributions to Greece

1981–2000 in million ECU and %

Year	*ECU million*	*as % of GDP*	*Year*	*ECU million*	*as % of GDP*
1981	132.7	0.28	1991	3,255.3	3.84
1982	561.4	1.01	1992	3,126.1	3.49
1983	937.1	1.69	1993	3,488.5	3.75
1984	906.1	1.49	1994	3,620.8	3.65
1985	1,138.9	1.82	1995	3,798.2	3.60
1986	1,414.3	2.47	1996	3,982.8	3.30
1987	1,442.7	2.54	1997	4,075.8	3.32
1988	1,636.1	2.54	1998	4,340.3	3.34
1989	2,361.5	2.29	1999*	4,034.4	3.03
1990	2,278.2	2.96	2000*	3,752.7	2.66
	Average	1.91		Average	3.39

*euros

Source Bank of Greece calculations; World Bank

period 1952–1955. In addition, Greece received two substantial medium-term loans to address balance of payments difficulties.

And what about trade? After all, this was the main reason for entering the Common Market. The evidence on this score is mixed. There is substantial evidence that there was a shift in the direction of trade favoring EEC countries in the first decade (see Table 5.4). The increase reflected in part the fact that Spain and Portugal joined the EU in 1983. The share of Greece's imports from the EU increased from 39.7% in 1980 to 64.1% in 1990. This involved both trade creation—i.e. increases in imports as a consequence of trade liberalization as well as trade diversion—i.e. increases in imports resulting from moving away from non-EU suppliers (Arghyrou, 2000, p. 157). The shift in the direction of exports was less pronounced but still substantial—from 47.6% to 63.9%. It appears to have resulted in an increase of Greece' share of Germany's and possibly UK's imports—both of whom however, were important markets for Greece (Arghyrou, 2000, p. 158).

As discussed earlier, the increased penetration of European imports presented challenges on Greek manufacturing production which was characterized by a multitude of small firms with low productivity growth. However, despite the problems, Greek exports of Apparel and Clothing

Table 5.4 Greece—Direction of trade 1980–2000

	In percent				
	1980	*1985*	*1990*	*1995*	*2000*
Imports					
European Union	39.7	46.7	64.1	69.9	56.4
Other OECD	24.4	16.7	16.8	9.7	17.0
Rest of World	35.9	36.6	19.1	20.4	26.6
Total	100.0	100.0	100.0	100.0	100.0
Exports					
European Union	47.6	53.4	63.9	60.7	43.8
Other OECD	10.2	16.4	15.1	9.0	16.4
Rest of World	42.8	30.2	21.0	30.3	39.8
Total	100.0	100.0	100.0	100.0	100.0

Note The composition of the above groupings changed considerably over the period: Spain and Portugal joined the EU in 1983; a number of OECD countries joined the EU in the 1990s (Austria, Finland and Sweden) and are included in the 1995 and 2000 EU estimates while some others (Mexico, Czech Republic, Hungary, Poland and South Korea) joined the OECD over the same period

Source Greece, National Statistical Service, *Statistical Yearbook*; UN COMTRADE

were still the largest Greek exports by value in 1990 and the second largest in 2000 and three quarters of them went to the EU (Table 5.5).

The decline in the importance of the EU market in the period 1990 to 2000 was due to two sets of factors: first, the very rapid increase of exports of finished petroleum products most of which were directed to destinations around the Mediterranean (Lebanon, Libya, Gibraltar). Greece is of course not an oil producer. But over time, Greece became home to a large refinery industry located near the coast. Crude oil would be imported, primarily from Iraq and Libya refined and re-exported. Second, following the fall of the Berlin wall over the decade of the 1990s, a number of new markets in the Balkans and Eastern Europe emerged for various Greek manufactures of machinery products and plastics. Agricultural exports however, declined in overall importance. From 26% of all exports in 1990, they fell to 18% in 2000. In all categories of agricultural exports, including tobacco and cotton, the share of exports that went to the EU fell over the decade (Table 5.5).

The impact on agriculture was more complex. Unlike manufacturing, Greece implemented the provisions of the CAP at the very beginning of its membership. The CAP at the time kept price supports higher than

Table 5.5 Greece: Top 10 exported commodities, and exports to EU, selected years

Code	Commodity	*Million US$ current prices and percent of Exports*															
		1990				*2000*				*2015*				*2020*			
		Rank	*Trade value*	*% of Exp.*	*EU %*	*Rank*	*Trade value*	*% of Exp.*	*EU %*	*Rank*	*Trade value*	*% of Exp.*	*EU %*	*Rank*	*Trade value*	*% of Exp.*	*·EU %*
3	Fish	29	56	0.7	91	16	214	2.0	93	10	647	2.3	92	11	820	2.3	90
8	Edible fruit	5	454	5.6	76	8	434	4.0	60	8	884	3.1	77	8	1269	3.6	74
15	Animal or vegetable fats and oils	9	303	3.8	90	13	248	2.3	81	9	829	2.9	85	14	659	1.9	81
20	Preparations of vegetables, fruit, nuts	2	597	7.4	68	6	472	4.4	53	7	1037	3.7	59	6	1329	3.8	50
24	Tobacco	8	336	4.2	43	9	389	3.6	24	16	499	1.8	48	15	628	1.8	51
-27	Mineral fuels, oils and products	3	583	7.3	40	1	1593	14.7	18	1	8431	29.8	26	1	7670	21.9	30
30	Pharmaceutical	26	64	0.8	57	14	230	2.2	81	4	1126	4.0	86	2	3279	9.4	72
39	Plastics	21	91	1.1	46	11	299	2.8	32	5	1103	3.9	66	7	1309	3.7	63
52	Cotton	7	409	5.1	70	7	465	4.3	44	17	381	1.4	15	18	486	1.4	9
61	Apparel and clothing	1	1013	12.6	74	2	991	9.1	77	19	365	1.3	93	19	476	1.4	85

(continued)

Table 5.5 (continued)

Code	*Commodity*	*Million US$ current prices and percent of Exports*															
		1990				*2000*				*2015*				*2020*			
		Rank	*Trade value*	*% of Exp.*	*EU %*	*Rank*	*Trade value*	*% of Exp.*	*EU %*	*Rank*	*Trade value*	*% of Exp.*	*EU %*	*Rank*	*Trade value*	*% of Exp.*	*EU %*
72	Iron and steel	6	447	5.5	76	19	172	1.6	58	18	369	1.3	52	16	542	1.8	64
76	Aluminum	10	295	3.7	76	4	506	4.7	55	2	1560	5.5	71	4	1839	5.2	73
84	Machinery	14	151	1.9	40	5	483	4.5	31	3	1395	4.9	56	3	1913	5.5	61
85	Electrical machinery	15	150	1.9	70	3	633	5.8	30	6	1054	3.7	72	5	1371	3.9	70
99	Unspecified	–	–	–	–	10	336	3.1	85	12	632	2.2	17	9	941	2.7	24

Source UN COMTRADE

world prices. "Since the poor tend to spend a larger proportion of their income on food, the burden of the CAP was regressive: poorer people and poorer countries carry a larger burden of the CAP. Thus when the poorer countries were added to the EEC (Ireland in 1973, Greece in 1981 and Spain and Portugal in 1985) the CAP caused significant transfers of income from consumers to producers, not only within the countries, but also from the newer poorer periphery to the core. The principal beneficiaries of the price supports were big farmers (in the EU North) who expanded production in response to guaranteed prices irrespective of market demand" (Oltheten et al., 2003, p. 782).

On balance the Greek experience with EEC membership in the first decade was a mix of successes and failures. Overall growth was stagnant as the expectations that I had that EEC entry would stimulate investment proved wrong. Investment as a portion of GDP remained stagnant at low levels hampering productivity growth and there was no significant increase in foreign direct investment inflows. The nationalization of industry did not help. Income distribution probably improved somewhat early on but not significantly later. On the success side one should count the financial support that Greece obtained from the Community at a time when it faced significant balance of payments and finance problems in large part as a result of its own doing. The trade side was mixed: there were significant pressures on the heavily protected manufacturing sector and export performance was less strong than anticipated. Agriculture did receive substantial supports but the impact on income distribution was not one that a government keen on helping the poor would want: the CAP was regressive helping the strong farmers primarily in Western Europe at the expense of poor consumers everywhere. By comparison to Portugal, which received roughly the same amount of EEC support, Greece transformed its export structure less, received far less private direct investment and its overall growth performance was significantly poorer while its income distribution was roughly comparable (Baer & Leite, 2003).

The Second Decade

The New Democracy government headed by K. Mitsotakis, that won the elections with a razor thin majority in April, 1990, faced a rapidly changing Europe. The fall of the Berlin wall in late 1989 had ushered a period of crumbling communist regimes in the Balkans and Eastern

Europe. Greece, traditionally a country of emigration, became the destination of thousands of refugees and illegal immigrants from surrounding countries. Domestically, the new government "received a country in an economic dead-end" (Iordanoglou, 2004, p. 27). There was a need to reduce substantially the budget deficit, as well as accommodate the inflow of immigrants and hopefully restart economic growth.

The new Greek government again sought the help of the EEC. In early 1991, it was able to obtain a new balance of payments loan of 2.2 billion ECU. The loan was to be disbursed in three tranches: 1.0 billion in March 1991 and 600 million ECU each in 1992 and 1993. The later tranches were conditioned on a huge number of prior actions and reforms ranging from the obvious and serious ones, such as the reduction of the borrowing requirement to no more than 10.4% in 1991 and 5% and 1.5% in 1993, to such details as: "The limitations on tourist expenditures…will be removed no later than two months from this decision" (EU, 1991). This is the kind of detailed conditionality that had been used from time to time in World Bank structural adjustment loans in the 1980s which had been justly criticized as being too intrusive and ineffective and had been largely abandoned by that time.

The government reduced the deficit from the 14–15% level of 1989–1990 to about 11.4% in 1991 (Iordanoglou, 2004, p. 14). It was also able to meet the borrowing requirement condition on the EEC loan in 1992 (Bank of Greece, 1993, p. 150). But progress in meeting the structural adjustment conditions was less than originally projected and the government decided not to seek the second tranche which had originally been scheduled for February 1992 (Bryant et al., 2001, p. 18). It also came no-where near to meeting the fiscal deficit reductions called for 1993. There were serious constraints in achieving these in part because of the increasing burden of servicing its debt.[4]

Internationally, following the 1991 reunification of Germany, Europe was moving forward toward greater integration which ultimately, led to the Maastricht Treaty of February, 1992 which was to become effective on November 1, 1993. The Treaty which Greece signed together with 11 other members of the EEC resulted in the establishment of the European Union with three pillars: (a) The European Community, (b) Common Foreign and Security Policy; and (c) cooperation in the fields of justice and home affairs. The European Community envisaged the creation of a European Monetary Union by 1999 and a single currency, the euro. However, it made membership conditional on the fulfillment of specific convergence criteria related to the country's budget deficit, outstanding debt and exchange rate performance before entry.

Greece was no-where near achieving these criteria. But the new PASOK government that won the early elections of October 1993, after a few months of indecision, became committed to attempt to meet the criteria of convergence. The first step was to defend the drachma which came under attack by speculators in early 1994. The Bank of Greece took the lead by setting prohibitively high interest rates which succeeded in protecting the drachma but also adversely affected economic activity. The government submitted a Revised Program of Convergence for 1994–1999 which was accepted by the EU Council in the fall of 1994.

The next several years reflected continued efforts at stabilizing the economy, including by generating surpluses on the primary government deficit in order to reduce the ratio of debt to GDP. The efforts became more pronounced following the 1996 elections which PASOK won again and the appointment of Simitis as Prime Minister. He felt that entry into the euro would have a beneficial effect both in restraining future pressures to run budget deficits, as there was a guideline that such deficits should not exceed 3% of GDP, and that the Greek private sector would benefit from access to lower cost credits.

In March, 1998 the drachma entered the EMS, devalued by 12.3% relative to the ECU and the country weathered successfully the international financial crisis of that year. In the next few months Greece entered the final stretch of the two-year period which was needed to meet the criteria for entering the monetary union on January 1, 2001.

The theory regarding the organization and participation in a monetary union was that, besides trade integration, it is most likely to succeed among countries with similar institutional and economic characteristics, including levels of development and production structures. And that, as an exchange rate adjustment would not be possible in case of asymmetric external shocks, it would be necessary to have alternatives, including labor mobility, wage-price flexibility and ultimately fiscal integration (Tavlas, 2019, p. 30). I would add that in the case of Greece, given the very large difference in development levels, another prerequisite would have been a commitment to provide capital transfers so that its economy would expand rapidly enough to converge over time with those of the rest of the Union.

During the last five years of the twentieth century the Greek economy recovered significantly. GDP growth rebounded to around 3.5% and there was substantial convergence toward the EU average. Inflation was contained and both private and public sector investment grew at around 9% per year, rates never achieved during the previous decade. A number of significant infrastructure projects were launched, including roads, the metro in the Athens area and a new airport.

Assistance from the EU continued throughout the decade. The average of net flows of Community funds for the period 1990–2000 amounted to 3.4% of GDP (see Table 5.3). The assistance became more focused on investment based on the '2nd Delors' package that was linked to the achievement of the Maastricht Treaty objectives. During the implementation of the package over the period 1994–1999, the total investment cost was 29.7 billion ECU, of which the EU funded 14.0 billion, the Greek government 7.1 billion and the private sector 8.7 billion (Manassani & Koltsidou, 2017). One of the new challenges of the Greek government was how to ensure that it was utilizing effectively the resources being made available to it through the European Union (Vasardani & Dimitropoulou, 2018).

The trade picture continued to present challenges: both exports and imports doubled in value over the decade of the 1990s but as the latter are double in value of the former, the current account deficit expanded significantly, both absolutely and relative to GDP (Table 5.1). The direction of Greek trade was affected by the break-up of the Soviet bloc and Greece increased both its exports and its imports with countries of Eastern Europe especially after the mid 1990s. The share of exports to the EU fell from 60.7% in 1995 to 43.8% in 2000, as the share of Germany declined by almost 10%, while the share of 'Other OECD' which during this period added Poland, Hungary, the Czech Republic and South Korea, rose from 9.0% in 1995 to 16.4% by the end of the century (Table 5.3). The share of imports from EU members and 'Other OECD' showed exactly the same changes as for exports.

As noted above, the composition of Greek exports continued to change. By the end of the decade, refined oil product exports became the number one export. Clothing and apparel continued to be of importance, in second place overall. Vegetables and Agricultural products, on the other hand declined in importance, with tobacco, so important in previous decades, falling to the ninth position (Table 5.5).

There were significant institutional reforms as well. A major reform involved the Bank of Greece: By a new law in 1997, it became the sole determinant of monetary policy. The independence of the Greek central bank was critical for the entry into the euro—although the entry would by itself result in a diminution of its powers. But there were other reforms as well, resulting from adherence to EU guidelines to reduce government monopolies and increase competition in transport and telecommunications, such as the privatization of Olympic Airways and opening up competition to the government monopoly of OTE (the major telecom provider); improve competition in the labor markets, technical standards affecting pollution and many others.

Indeed, it could be argued that the major benefit accruing to Greece from its EU membership was that, "Common EU policies can be very helpful in facilitating structural reforms in small peripheral economies, such as Greece. However, these policies must be continuously evaluated and improved so that their effectiveness is maximized" (Olthelten et al., p. 775).

Still, there were many institutional weaknesses which could (should?) have given policy makers some concern about the difficulties of participating in the monetary union. In the late 1990s Greece ranked considerably below the EU average in the World Bank governance indicators that affect social and economic interactions (Christodoulakis, 2019, p. 10). These institutions play an important role both in determining long-term growth and responses to external shocks. In particular, the concerns related to: (a) Government effectiveness, including the quality, effectiveness and degree of independence from political pressures of the civil service; the quality of policy formulation and implementation, and the credibility of Government's commitment to such policies; (b) The Government's ability to formulate and implement sound policies and regulations that permit and promote private sector activities and developments; (c) The rule of law, i.e. the extent to which people have confidence in, and abide by, the legal provisions of the society, in particular, the quality of contract enforcement, property rights and the functioning of courts; and (d) the extent of corruption and the 'capturing' of the state by elites and private[5] interests. But the criteria for convergence focused more narrowly on the government's effectiveness and commitment to policies that affected macroeconomic performance.

A Somber Assessment of the Greek Government's Capacity for Reform

Most attempts to restructure Greece since the 1990s failed because of the rise of statist ideology aided by the permeation of the state by political parties, which allowed corruption and patronage to run rampant in the country. As a result, capacity diminished in public administration at a time when the government gladly accepted more responsibilities to implement EU directives. Attempts to realign capacity to responsibility failed because of resistance by the same public sector employees whom politicians hired in the first place. The fear of losing benefits in a non-meritocratic system took away any incentives on the part of employees of all political persuasions to accept possible losses, even when they agreed with reforms (Kalaitzidis & Zahariades, 2015, p. 16).

The result was that by the beginning of 2000 Greece was judged to have met the criteria for entry into the euro: Inflation had dropped to around 2.5%, the budget deficit was less than 3% the debt ratio was becoming manageable, and the drachma had stayed within the EMS for a duration of two years without being devalued. The convergence criteria proved to be a successful mechanism to achieve—at least for a time, macroeconomic stability in Greece, a country with a poor historical record. At the EU Summit in Portugal's Santa Maria de Feira on June 19–20, Greece was formally admitted into the euro effective January 1, 2001, with the drachma exchange rate to euro at 340.75:1. And so started a new era of dependence.

Notes

1. Given the significant shadow economy, changes in the Gini coefficients should be interpreted with caution.
2. Medium-term loans by the EEC at the time had 2–5 year maturity.
3. Garganas (2024, p. 38) who was in the Papandreou government at the time states that, "The strict implementation of the 1985 stabilization program over the two succeeding years was a landmark." A similar claim is made in Bryant et al. (2001, p. 16). As noted above, the conditionality was only partly met but the EC was happy enough for the limited progress made to release the second tranche.

4. The last two tranches were apparently never disbursed. The Bank of Greece annual reports which typically record such loans speak only of the Government foreign borrowing through the issuance of bonds in 1992 and 1993.
5. There are weaknesses in these Indicators as discussed in Christodoulakis (2019, pp. 12–13) and they have been discontinued since 2021. But the issues they refer to have been the subject of concern for as long as Greece has been independent.

References

Alogoskoufis, G. (2021). *Historical Cycles of the Economy of Modern Greece from 1821 to the Present* (Hellenic Observatory, LSE, Paper 158).

Arghyrou, M. G. (2000). EU Participation and the External Trade of Greece: An Appraisal of the Evidence. *Applied Economics, 32*(2), 151–159.

Baer, W., & Leite, A. N. (2003). The economy of Portugal within the European Union: 1990–2002. *Quarterly Review of Economics and Finance, 43*(2003), 738–754.

Bank of Greece. (1985). *President's Report for 1985*. Bank of Greece.

Bank of Greece. (1987). *President's Report for 1987*. Bank of Greece.

Bank of Greece. (1993). *President's Report for 1993*. Bank of Greece.

Bank of Greece. (2024). *EU Net Transfers to Greece: 1981–2023, Calculations*. mimeo . Bank of Greece.

Bryant, R. C., et al. (2001). Introduction. In R. C. Bryant, N. C. Garganas, & G. S. Tavlas (Eds.), *Greece's Economic Performance and Prospects*. Bank of Greece and Brookings Institution.

Christodoulakis, N. (2019). *Greece and the Euro Area: The Cost of Weak Institutions* (Working Paper Series 19-08). Athens University of Economics and Business.

EU Council. (1985). *EC Official Journal* L341 19/12/1985 p.0017-0018-85/543/EEC Council Decision.

EU Council. (1991). *EC Official Journal* L065 13/03/1991 p.0022-0024-91/136/EEC Council Decision.

Garganas, N. (2024). *Greece's Sovereign Debt Crisis and Its Economic Aftermath: Analysis and Lessons*. Kerkyra Pablications.

Iordanoglou, X. I. (2004). The Economy in the Period 1974–2000: Deceleration, Stagnation and Recovery. In B. Panayotopoulos (Ed.), *History of the New Hellenic Nation* (Vol. 10) (in Greek- Athens: Editions Greek Letters-Εκδοσεις Ελληνικα Γραμματα).

Kalaitzidis, A., & Zahariadis, N. (2015). Greece's Trouble with European Union Accession. *Cahiers de la Méditerranée* [Online], 90 | 2015, Online Since 01 December 2015, Connection on 08 September 2020. http://journals.openedition.org/cdlm/7951

Manassani, A., & Koltsidou, E. (2017). *The Contribution of EU Transfers to Greece's Balance of Payments and Economic Development* (#2 pp. 235–260). Bank of Greece (in Greek).

Mitrakos, Th., & Tsakloglou, P. (2011). *Inequality, Poverty and Material Well-being: From the Restoration of Democracy to the Current Crisis*. Bank of Greece Conference on "Social policies and social cohesion in light of the current economic crisis", Bank of Greece.

Oltheten, E., et al. (2003). Greece in the European Union: Policy Lessons from Two Decades of Membership. *Quarterly Review of Economics and Finance, 43*, 774–806.

Spraos, J. (2001). EU Transfers and Greece's Real Exchange Rate: A Naked Eye View. In R. C. Bryant, N. C. Garganas, & G. S. Tavlas (Eds.), *Greece's Economic Performance and Prospects*. Bank of Greece and Brookings Institution.

Tavlas, G. (2019). *The Theory of Monetary Integration in the Aftermath of the Greek Financial Crisis*. The Seventh Lectio Minghetti. IBL Libri.

Vasardani, M., & Dimitropoulou, D. (2018, July). The Utilization of EU Structural Funds in Greece, Bank of Greece. *Economic Bulletin, 54*, 34–48.

Voulgaris, G. (2008). *Greece during the Restoration of Democracy* (in Greek "Η Ελλάδα της μεταπολίτευσης 1974–1990"). Themelio.

wider.unu.edu/database/world-income-inequality-database-wiid

CHAPTER 6

Euphoria and Bust

Introduction

When I moved from Brussels to Athens in early July 2001, seven months after the introduction of the euro, I found a city bustling with energy and optimism. There was a new airport, and there was construction everywhere including expansion of the metro. A new ring road was being built cutting commuter time in half and the narrow two-lane highway to Marathon was becoming a four-lane thoroughfare that was to be completed before the Olympics—three years hence, so that the race could be properly run in the original route. There was the usual grumbling: the introduction of the euro had given the opportunity for merchants to raise prices. And, of course, there were the usual hassles with the bureaucracy: the registration of my imported car required 27 signatures from various agencies although it was coming in duty-free from another EU country and could only be accomplished by paying 500 euros to a 'facilitator.'

The euphoria peaked in the summer of 2004. At that time, the Greek national soccer team unexpectedly won the European Championship, and later that summer, the city glowed in the brilliance of a memorable Olympics. The good feelings lasted for a while after the Olympics. As usual, there was little hint of the problems that were lurking and would envelop the country in the next few years. This chapter will review briefly the first few years of the twenty-first century and then turn to a discussion

C. Michalopoulos, *Greek Foreign Trade and Finance*, Palgrave Studies in Economic History, https://doi.org/10.1007/978-3-031-92104-9_6

of the causes of the crisis that started in 2009 and the reasons why the crisis was so deep and protracted.

The Boom Years

There is an immense literature about the euro and the Greek debt crisis that will not be discussed in detail here. The literature contains a number of different original sins according to the writer's, sometimes politically colored, perspective. First, there was the view shared by many economists that the original sin was the establishment of the euro, which was doomed to fail sooner, or later. The reasons advanced included the unwillingness of the more productive and better-governed group of countries in the North, to make transfers to the South (Friedman, 1997). Another reason was that a fiscal union should have preceded the monetary union. Dornbush (1996) concluded, "If there was ever a bad idea, a European Monetary Union is it." A variation on this is that the eurozone, as structured at the time could not accommodate members with significantly different cultures, economic policies, institutions and productivity levels—and that this should have been understood before permitting Greece to join. Others simply believed that Greece should not have been permitted to join the euro, as it cheated by producing fake statistics that enabled it to meet eurozone criteria at entry. Another perspective lays the blame on the private capital market, which exhibit herd behavior based on incomplete information (Michalopoulos, 2017, pp. 241–243).

The facts are as follows. The balance of payments had changed little: The current account had been in deficit consistently for more than fifty years. However, with the exceptions of the crises in 1985 and 1991, it had been managed effectively and rarely exceeded 5% of GDP, primarily because the Bank of Greece had typically had good and steady leadership. However, in 2001–2005 the current account deficit grew in parallel with the budget deficit: from around 7% of GDP in 2001–2005, it exploded to 14% in 2007–2008 (Table 6.1).

The composition of exports continued the trends of the previous decade. Petroleum products continued to be the biggest exports, based on crude oil imports from the Middle-East refined in Greece. Exports of textiles and clothing continued to be important but declining over time, to be replaced by pharmaceuticals and metal products. Agricultural products continued their decline dropping to 15% of the total in 2005 and only 10% in 2012 (see Table 6.2).

Table 6.1 Greece—Summary balance of payments

	Million US$ current prices and percent								
	2000	*2005*	*2008*	*2011*	*2013*	*2015*	*2018*	*2020*	*2023*
Imports-Goods	30,321	51,680	93,769	65,381	63,316	47,121	64,741	54,171	88,500
Exports-Goods	10,120	17,462	28,869	27,471	35,700	27,518	38,208	33,036	53,465
Net Services	7917	19,139	25,440	20,560	20,871	18,383	22,597	8398	23,763
CA Balance	−9817	−18,219	−51,297	−28,599	−4949	−1611	−6249	−12,413	−15,056
CA/GDP	−7.5%	−7.4%	−14.4%	−10.1%	−2.0%	−0.8%	−3.0%	−6.6%	−6.3%

Source World Bank WDI

The share of Greek exports that went to the EU market rose from the low point of 2000, in part because of the addition of new members into the EU in 2004 and 2007, but never reached the high levels of dependence of the 1980s and 1990s. The same holds true for imports (see Table 6.3). Indeed, it would appear that in 2012, as the Greek economy was in deep recession, the share of imports of consumer products from the EU fell to its lowest point in decades (45.1%) and has not significantly expanded since (Table 6.3). This is partly because of the continued importance of oil imports for the Greek refinery sector, but also more generally from the reorientation of the Greek economy to imports from non-EU markets. The share of non-EU OECD, which means distant markets such as in the US, Canada, Australia, South Korea, Mexico and more recently Costa Rica has varied little in the range of 13–19% for both exports and imports.

The trade balance continued to have a large deficit not fully offset by a significant surplus on services, mainly shipping and tourism. The resulting deficit was financed by borrowing in the private capital markets, which supported a robust GDP growth of close to 4% per year between 2000 and 2005. This level of debt issuance at spreads that were only slightly higher than the German benchmark was only possible because creditors viewed Greek debt as Eurozone debt, and this complacency by the markets encouraged the Greek government to over-borrow. Then came a period of massive current account deficits in 2005–2008, further borrowing, until the roof caved in during 2009 (Table 6.4).

Throughout the period Eurozone assistance continued, seemingly unaffected by developments in the Greek economy. As Table 6.5 shows,

Table 6.2 Greece: top 10 exported commodities, selected years

Code	Commodities	*Million US$ and percent of Exports* 1995			2005			2012			2018			2023		
		Rank	*Trade value*	*% of Exp.*	*Rank*	*Trade value*	*% of Exp.*	*Rank*	*Trade value*	*% of exports*	*Rank*	*Trade value*	*% of Exp.*	*Rank*	*Trade value*	*% of Exp.*
3	Fish	19	151	1.4	15	420	2.9	10	768	2.2	11	801	2.0	12	1013	1.8
8	Edible Fruit	6	511	4.7	10	571	3.3	8	978	2.8	9	1055	2.7	9	1543	2.8
15	Animal fats and oils	5	612	5.6	12	500	2.9	14	552	1.6	10	852	2.2	8	1589	2.9
20	Preparations of vegetables fruits and nuts	4	633	5.8	8	651	3.7	6	1128	3.2	6	1239	3.1	6	1677	3.1
24	Tobacco	8	405	3.7	11	530	3.0-	15	550	1.6	17	577	1.5	13	1005	1.9
27	Mineral fuels, oils and products	2	713	6.5	1	1642	9.4	1	13,691	38.9	1	13,556	34.3	1	17,815	32.4
30	Pharmaceutical	28	78	0.7	2	1169	6.7	4	1237	3.5	4	1732	4.4	2	3025	5.5
39	Plastics	16	204	1.9	7	796	4.6	5	1154	3.3	5	1392	3.5	7	1648	3.0
52	Cotton	3	652	6.0	9	586	3.4	13	655	1.9	18	458	1.2	22	480	0.9
61	Apparel and clothing	1	1270	11.6	3	1092	6.3	18	459	1.3	19	456	1.2	25	457	0.8
72	Iron and steel	12	360	3.3	16	401	2.3	9	816	2.3	14	750	1.9	18	610	1.1
76	Aluminum	7	504	4.6	5	926	5.3	2	1539	4.4	2	2068	5.2	3	2720	4.9
84	Machinery	5	483	4.5	6	856	4.9	7	981	2.8	3	1875	4.8	5	2368	4.3

Code	Commodities	*Million US$ and percent of Exports* 1995			2005			2012			2018			2023		
		Rank	*Trade value*	*% of Exp.*	*Rank*	*Trade value*	*% of Exp.*	*Rank*	*Trade value*	*% of exports*	*Rank*	*Trade value*	*% of Exp.*	*Rank*	*Trade value*	*% of Exp.*
85	Electrical machinery	10	392	3.6	4	950	5.4	3	1375	3.9	7	1176	3.0	4	2378	4.3
99	Unspecified Commodities	17	201	1.8	13	447	2.6	12	714	2.0	8	1067	2.7	11	1183	2.2

Data Source UN COMTRADE

Table 6.3 Greek Direction of trade 2000–2023

	In percent						
	2000	*2005*	*2008*	*2012*	*2015*	*2020*	*2023*
Exports							
European Union	43.8	53.1	59.6	43.0	53.3	56.2	56.1
Other OECD	16.4	13.7	12.9	19.4	16.6	17.9	16.9
Rest of World	39.8	33.2	27.5	37.6	30.1	25.1	27.0
Total	100.0	100.0	100.0	100.0	100.0	100.0	100.0
Imports							
European Union	56.4	56.2	55.2	45.1	51.8	54.2	47.2
Other OECD	16.4	13.7	12.9	19.4	16.6	17.9	16.9
Rest of World	31.8	33.2	27.5	37.6	30.1	25.1	27.0
Total	100.0	100.0	100.0	100.0	100.0	100.0	100.0

Source UN COMTRADE

Table 6.4 Greece growth rates, GFC and EU transfers 2000–2023

	In percent at constant 2015 prices		
	GDP Growth	*GFC/GDP*	*Net EU/GDP*
2000–2008	3.6	20.7	2.3
2008–2013	−5.0	15.7	2.1
2013–2018	0.0	11.2	2.4
2018–2023	1.7	12.6	2.9

Sources World Bank, Bank of Greece

the amount of assistance relative to GDP varied considerably during the period 2001–2012. It was significantly higher during the boom years to 2008 and it fell substantially during the period of the deepest crisis 2009–2012, only to rise again later on. EU funded investment only accounted for about 4% of GFC; but it fell to almost nothing during the lean years.

A series of public sector deficits ran by the previous two governments culminated in 2009. The Karamanlis (New Democracy) government that ran the country since 2004 definitely produced the largest ones.[1] In all cases, the programmed deficits were supposed to be less than 3% of GDP, consistent with the Maastricht guidelines. In all cases, they exceeded the target: they rose from 3.2% in 2000 to 7.2% in 2004 (the year of the Athens Olympics), were in excess of 5% in 2005–2007 and more than

Table 6.5 EU transfers to Greece 2001–2023

Year	*In million euro and %*			
	Total (net)	*% of GDP*	*Capital flows*	*% of GFC*
2001	4,071.8	2.68	2,140.9	5.13
2002	3,762.3	2.30	1,617.3	5.56
2003	3,205.7	1.29	1,211.9	4.40
2004	4,257.6	2.30	2,394.1	3.94
2005	3,808.2	1.91	2,114.2	4.08
2006	5,074.0	2.33	3,084.4	3.86
2007	4,910.1	2.11	4,374.4	0.89
2008	6,011.0	2.48	4,049.9	3.40
2009	2,967.1	1.25	2,118.8	1.72
2010	2,551.8	1.14	2,223.7	0.88
2011	3,555.3	1.75	2,785.8	2.77
2012	3,854.6	2.00	2,472.3	6.50
2013	7,266.8	4.04	3,289.2	19.75
2014	5,221.5	3.95	2,781.0	12.71
2015	4,668.2	2.66	2,315.2	12.39
2016	3,230.1	1.85	1,169.7	10.73
2017	2,687.4	1.52	1,037.2	7.91
2018	2,759.1	1.54	623.4	10.67
2019	4,135.3	2.26	1,018.1	15.91
2020	6,308.1	3.82	2,927.5	16.95
2021	8,278.4	4.56	4,050.5	17.50
2022	5,033.3	2.44	2,516.0	8.40
2023	6,615.7	3.00	2,817.8	12.42

Sources Bank of Greece calculations and World Bank

9% in 2008. Some of this spending is attributable to large expenditures on pensions, where the replacement rate was much higher than in other Eurozone countries. Another part had to do with increased government payrolls by converting temporary employees to permanent civil servants. And there were large deficits in the public sector hospitals. Despite the deficits and because of the rapid GDP growth, the 113% ratio of public debt to Greek GDP in 2008 was only marginally higher than the 111% debt/GDP in 1996. However, a great deal of the debt had a short maturity structure posing significant dangers of future default.

It was clear to the founders of the EMU that some coordination on fiscal policy was essential for its survival, and that is why they set up the 3% budget deficit rule. When both Germany and France committed sins by violating the rule with impunity in the early years of the twenty-first century, they jeopardized the credibility of the rules—as unobserved rules are no rules at all, and rules enforced only on the weak members lead to resentment and non-observance. "The EMU contained two construction deffects which can be summarized in two asymmetries: the asymmetry between a complete monetary union and an incomplete economic union; and the asymmetry between monetary integration and the lack of centralized financial supervision, i.e. a banking union" (Lazaretou, 2021, p. 2).

"There was also massive private credit expansion after 2000, as the Eurozone real interest rates were much lower than what had prevailed in Greece for decades. A mortgage market also emerged for the first time to help satisfy the Greek desire for second homes. However, the building bubble was nowhere near the levels reached in Ireland and Spain. Credit cards became common where none had existed before and the economy as a whole was booming until 2008. The ratio of private sector loans to GDP stood at 34% in 1998 before entry to the Eurozone. At the time, this was about half of what it was in Italy, and slightly more than a third of Portugal and Ireland. As of 2008, private sector debt had more than tripled, to 103% of GDP and was higher than Italy's– although still lower than Ireland and Portugal. Typically, when credit expansion is so much faster than GDP growth, trouble looms ahead" (Michalopoulos, 2017, pp. 244–245).

In addition, the ECB's monetary policy aggravated asymmetric financial flows. Due to divergent fiscal and incomes policies, it was difficult for the ECB to conduct a monetary policy appropriate for all Member States. In fact, monetary policy proved to be excessively loose for the debtor countries and overheating economies of the euro periphery. Credit expansion funded by cheap capital inflows fed a consumption bubble and asset price inflation. It also pushed inflation higher in the periphery well above rates in core euro area countries.

"The persistently high inflation in the periphery led to lower real interest rates, compared to higher real rates in the core countries. Inflation and real interest rate divergence encouraged capital flows into the periphery, which went to non-tradable sectors, while at the same time they increased savings and fueled current account surpluses in the core countries. Ultimately, this asymmetric operation of EMU led to an appreciation of the real exchange rate in the peripheral debtor countries, resulting in a gradual erosion of their competitiveness. Conversely, the core creditor countries experienced increased savings and lower inflation rates, leading to a depreciation of their real exchange rates and an improvement of their competitiveness" (Lazaretou, 2021 pp. 2–3). The private capital market however, ignored these large differences and on the eve of the crisis Greek borrowing costs were only slightly higher than those in Germany.

The Bust

The details of the onset of the 2009 crisis are well known. As soon as the Papandreou[2] (PASOK) government came to power following the October 2009 parliamentary election, it became clear that the budget deficit, which was thought to be in the neighborhood of 6% of GDP, was likely to be around 12% (Papaconstantinou, 2015, p. 32). Later, the estimate was increased to 13.6% with the final number reaching 15.4%.[3]

"In January 2010, the Greek government floated five-year bonds for 5 billion euro at 6.2%. The offering was oversubscribed and resulted in borrowings of 8 billion euro. However, this would not be enough. In the next two months the markets started to focus on the financing needs of the Greek economy resulting in credit rating downgrades and increases in borrowing costs. A serious problem was emerging, as without help Greece would have had to default on existing obligations" (see also Gibson et al., 2014). This is where the three major actors in this modern tragedy, the Greek Government, its Eurozone partners and the IMF entered the scene and started to commit their sins.[4]

The debt problem was not without precedent. In the 1980s and 1990s, many developing countries, some with very large economies—albeit with slightly lower per capita incomes, had faced similar problems and had sought assistance from the IMF. The international community had taken a long time, at considerable cost to the economies concerned to come up with a solution. "By 1986 informed opinion understood that Third World Debt would have to be reduced, written off, defaulted" (Galbraith, 2016, p. 52). But it took the international community three more years to launch the Brady bond schemes which helped bail out more than a dozen middle-income countries (and more than a decade later for official debts of poor countries). Successful programs had several common characteristics:

- There was invariably an IMF program to restore macroeconomic balances, usually involving tight monetary policy a reduction in budget deficits and overall absorption, which resulted in temporary contraction of output and reduced employment.

- There was a program of structural adjustment, usually involving a number of measures that would reorient production toward exportables, through a real exchange rate depreciation (often a substantial nominal devaluation combined with trade policy reforms), and a number of other structural reforms usually monitored by the World Bank—which would also provide additional longer-term financial support.
- Few conditions were supposed to be attached to the programs and they were supposed to be measurable and focused on important aspects of reforms.
- Government ownership of the reform program was critical to its success as was its ability to convince public opinion about the necessity of the proposed reforms
- Foreign Private Debt was reduced: outstanding debt obligations to foreign private bond-holders would be reduced through the exchange of the maturing debt with new debt of lower nominal value resulting in losses to private sector bond-holders; the latter were forced to accept such losses in exchange for the greater certainty of the reforming countries servicing the new debt. Last, and perhaps most important, the debt reduction was to be of such magnitude as to restore the capacity of the reforming country to service it over time, i.e. it was to meet the debt sustainability test.

In early 2010, the Greek government engaged in a series of tortuous negotiations with its Eurozone partners who initially were not keen in having the IMF participate in a rescue of a Eurozone country. Later, following a shift in the German position, the IMF was brought in resulting in another set of negotiations with the Troika (i.e. the European Commission, the European Central Bank and the IMF). After a final set of discussions with the IMF, which had problems in participating in the rescue for a variety of reasons, including the projected debt profile for the Greek debt and the size of the borrowing from the IMF, agreement was reached in May 2010 on a two-year program of support. The program involved credits of 110 billion euro (80 million from bilateral loans by Eurozone governments and 30 million from the IMF).

Fake Statistics?
The fake statistics issue received prominence in 2010 when it became apparent that the previous Greek government had substantially underreported the 2009 budget deficit. Eurostat was brought in to assess the Greek budget and debt statistics. It found a very large under reporting of the budget deficit and *inter alia* that the government had not reported a series of foreign exchange swaps it had undertaken in 2001 with Goldman Sachs as well as a number of related interest rate swaps it had concluded with the same company which were recapitalized later. This resulted in the under reporting of outstanding debt by about 5.4 billion euros or 2.2% of GNP in 2010. However, at the time the original arrangements were made, in 2001, the Eurostat rules defining government debt specifically excluded swaps—as well as other forms of financial derivatives. In 2008, the rules were changed and the Greek government failed to report the debt at the time as it should have (Eurostat, 2010). However, the critical point is different: The swaps were undertaken in 2001. By that time, Greece already had been admitted to the euro based on a decision of the EU Summit of 2000 using statistics for 1999 (Sardelis, 2013).

The terms of the loans were onerous: three years at around 5% for the European government loans with a half point additional for the 'service' provided, and slightly lower interest rates for the IMF. "It was decided to set punitively high interest rates in order to reassure those who considered that financial assistance was a dangerous encouragement of lax policies" (Pisani-Ferry, 2014, p. 9). There was a memorandum of understanding containing the agreed reforms including prior conditions and benchmarks. However, there was no reduction of private sector debt, which was a fateful omission that doomed the program.

It was agreed that the Greek government would implement a very large up-front reduction of the budget deficit from what was originally thought to be 13.6% of GDP to 9%. It was projected that GDP would decline for a year or two but growth would be restored in 2012 as would access to the private markets enabling Greece to repay the official credits and the IMF in short order as well as restore long-term debt sustainability. The IMF credit at 3,200% of Greece's IMF quota was the largest ever provided relative to the member's quota. The credit was provided despite staff misgivings about the projected debt sustainability.

The very large IMF credit "required a modification of the Fund's exceptional access policy framework, but the need for a policy change was not disclosed to the (IMF) Board until the staff report had been circulated. The policy change was embedded in the report requesting the Greek Stand-By Arrangement, and therefore was to be implicitly approved along with the formal and explicit request for Fund resources" (IMF, 2017, p. vii; Wyplosz & Sgherri, 2016). "The justification for the policy change was that in the absence of the credit, there was 'systemic' risk, resulting from the possibility that the Greek problems would result in 'contagion' for other Eurozone countries, which would face difficulties in rolling over their large private market borrowings" (Michalopoulos, 2017, pp. 245–247).

Was the systemic exemption a mistake? Should the IMF have insisted on the restructuring of Greek debt at the outset of the program, instead of invoking this exemption? The answer is not straightforward. Ultimately, it depends on the objectives of the program. If the objective was to help Greece, the country that had requested assistance, then the answer is simple. Instead of the adopted program, the IMF should have insisted on a program that included a restructuring of the debt. In his May 2010 Spiegel interview, Karl Otto Pohl argued that Greek debt should have been restructured, to reduce it by one third. Asked about the program, Pohl disputed official explanations, which had been advanced by Chancellor Merkel's government, about its rationale and observed: "It was about protecting German banks, but especially the French banks, from debt write offs" (Orphanides, 2015, p. 11).

Though the previous experiences with debt problems under the Brady scheme pointed to the need for a private sector debt write-down, apparently, it was not considered. This was a fundamental flaw, which would cause problems down the line—a conclusion shared by all serious analysts (Baldwin & Giavazzi, 2016, p. 55).

Not that there was no concern about the possibility of Greek default. However, the focus of the Eurozone and the ECB was not to help address the Greek problem, but rather to protect the German, French and Dutch banks that held large amounts of Greek debt.

At about the same time as the announcement of the Greek program in May 2010 the ECB, under the direction of its governor Jean Paul Trichet, former governor of the Bank of France, initiated the Securities Market Program (SMP) under which it bought large quantities of bonds at significant discount issued by Greece, Spain and Portugal. The program was ostensibly focused on 'repairing the monetary transmission mechanism' whatever that may mean. In fact, it was about the strong Eurozone members protecting their banks (Tavlas, 2019, p. 58).[5]

The Greek program was 'on track' from May to October 2010. It the fall of 2010 it became apparent that the very large up-front reduction in the Greek budget deficit of 5.5% would not be enough to produce the desired target deficit of less than 3% by 2014 as the actual 2009 deficit turned out to be even larger by an additional 1.8% of GDP.[6] This would necessitate even greater austerity in the second year of the program. The Merkel-Sarkozy Deauville agreement in late 2010 to modify the Eurozone understanding in ways that could result in significant losses to private sector holders of official debt in case of a Eurozone country default led to further weakening of the prospects of Greece's returning to the markets in the near future.[7]

Similarities and Differences: Previous Sovereign Debt Crises and Greece

The failure to resolve the Greek debt problem after two years of efforts by the international community raised questions as to its uniqueness. In fact, there were significant similarities and some differences between debt crises in the 1980s and 1990s and the Greek bailouts:

"First, debt levels in Greece were twice than the average of a sample of 57 economies that experienced some kind of debt crisis in the period 1980–2014, but not significantly different from Ireland, Italy, Portugal and Spain or some of the larger earlier defaults (Gourinchas et al., 2016, p. 3).

Second, the crisis in Greece involved a combination of sovereign debt default, a boom/bust cycle in foreign borrowing and a sudden stop in such borrowing in 2010. This combination had only been present on nine other occasions in emerging markets (Gourinchas et al., 2016, p. 64).

Third, of these ten most difficult cases, only in one other occasion (Argentina, 2001) did the country attempt for a limited time to undertake an adjustment through internal devaluation. Internal devaluation meant that competitiveness was to be restored and the current account improve, not through exchange rate adjustment, but through relative declines in costs and prices of exportables. Unlike the other debt relief programs in developing countries, Greece was not a master of its own monetary, exchange rate and trade policies. ECB determined monetary policy. It alone could decide the amounts of credit it would make available to Greek banks. As a member of the EU customs union and the Eurozone, Greece did not have the option of fixing or not fixing its exchange rate or change its trade policies in order to effect a real exchange rate depreciation; it had to rely on internal devaluation through changes in the domestic level of prices and wages.[8] Fourth, the original Greek bailout did not involve a PSI (Private Sector Involvement), which would have reduced outstanding debt. There was a PSI in the second bailout. However, in the meantime, the private sector, mainly commercial banks in Germany and France were able to unload about 40 billion euro of Greek debt. They unloaded another 10 billion euro, while the second bailout was being negotiated, and thus forced a greater burden of the haircut on Greek domestic banks, which had to be recapitalized, as well as on Greek pension funds.

Fifth, unlike most emerging countries benefiting from the Brady schemes who were only able to obtain support from the IFIs, Greece, as a member of the Eurozone could ask and did obtain substantial financial assistance from its Eurozone partners.[9] On the other hand, Greece's participation in the Eurozone increased the politicization of both the reform package and the bailouts as well as increased the complexity of reaching agreement between the Troika and Greece.

Finally, although Greece's per capita income was higher than the typical Brady country, Greece's governance, business practices, regulations, judicial system and many of its institutions were not significantly different from those of higher middle-income developing countries" (Michalopoulos, 2017, pp. 248–249).

Failures to Heed Lessons of the Past

The Eurozone

"The governments of the Eurozone countries and the ECB were dead set against a PSI and debt reduction from the outset of the negotiations." They were in part concerned about the impact of a PSI on the health of the banking system especially in France and Germany, which had just started to emerge from the problems of the financial meltdown of late 2008. It has been argued that their main concern was not with the impact of a PSI in a Greek rescue as such but the precedent it would set for other Eurozone countries, in particular, Italy and Spain in which European banks had even larger portfolios. They agreed to a PSI in Greece later on, by which time their banking system had shed the bulk of the Greek debt and they had had time to put together a more formal defense mechanism for eurozone countries needing assistance. Greece thus became the 'perfect culprit' in Pisani-Ferry's term (Pisani-Ferry, 2014) or 'sacrificial lamb' (Stiglitz, 2015) to maintain Eurozone cohesion and avoid problems with bigger countries.

It was also claimed that a PSI could not have been done as long as Jean-Paul Trichet was President of the ECB (Papaconstantinou, 2016, p. 254). In his previous career as Deputy Chair of the Paris Club in 1982–1985 he presided over dozens of official debt reschedulings, often on hard terms and no debt reductions.

Finally, it is alleged that Eurozone members gave private assurances to other members of the IMF governing board at its crucial meeting in April 2010 deciding the IMF support of the Greek bailout that they would urge their private banks to maintain their exposure in Greece (Orphanides, 2015). It is not known whether they did or not. But, even if they did, the lesson of the 1980s was clear: government entreaties to the private sector banks to maintain or increase exposure to highly indebted countries fall on deaf ears. Only debt reduction packages do. This did not materialize in the first bailout, as it should have. Greece was saddled with a very large official debt on onerous terms that has become a major constraint to its future growth. Reductions in its nominal value or its terms would entail formal budgetary losses to European governments that are always politically difficult and even more so today.

The IMF

A lot has been made about the way the IMF decided to participate in the first bailout: that proper procedure for such a size drawing was not followed, that warnings about debt sustainability were not heeded and that the Eurozone IMF Board members pressured others in light of their own participation in the aid package (Wyplosz & Sgherri, 2016). It can also be argued that Dominique Strauss-Kahn, IMF Managing Director at the time, wanted Greece to get an IMF standby because he wanted to show the IMF relevance in resolving a systemic crisis only a year after the IMF had undergone a substantial downsizing because many of its important members no longer thought it useful.[10]

My concerns are more substantive: the IMF staff projections under the first (as well as the second bailout) did not take into account the known and knowable facts about the Greek situation in making the projections of recovery and debt sustainability. There were problems with at least three aspects of the program: the multiplier used to estimate the real impact of the proposed reduction in the budget deficit; the implications of an internal devaluation for output and employment; and the nature and impact of the structural adjustment conditions attached to the program. To its credit, the IMF recognized some of these weaknesses later on (IEO, 2016; IMF, 2017). Unfortunately, they were not taken into consideration of the second IMF program in 2012.

Regarding the multiplier used, it was clearly too low as it did not take into account the fact that Greece's tradeables sector is a relatively small part of the economy (Bowerm et al., 2014). This meant that the projected impact of the deficit reduction on GDP was much smaller than the one actually observed.

Moreover, the impact of the internal devaluation on real output was equally underestimated. The IMF staff had at its disposal the extensive experience of West Africa where internal devaluation efforts led to massive GDP reductions over several years. Was it because the West African countries were poorer and smaller economies and hence were not considered relevant? Was it because the French government and the ECB did not want to focus attention on the experience in West Africa where Trichet as head of the French Treasury opposed the devaluation of the West African Franc for many years to the detriment of the countries concerned?[11] In Greece, the actual real exchange rate depreciation was only 4.5% between 2008 and 2014, compared with 10% for the average country facing a sudden stop in its lending and 35% for countries experiencing the massive problems of Greece (Gourinchas et al., 2016). Given the low price elasticity for Greek exports (see below), it is not at all surprising that the adjustment of the current account resulted almost exclusively from contraction in imports which was related to the overall contraction of demand and GDP.

In any case, as an IMF assessment admits, had these factors been taken into account, it would have required a more gradual deficit reduction, which would have required more financial assistance to make the program workable. This would have required either more money from the Eurozone members or significantly softer terms that would have undercut their efforts to show that 'profligate' countries such as Greece should expect to be punished not rewarded for their bad policies.

The conditionality on the structural side contained more conditions than usual because it was judged, correctly, that Greece had a weak institutional capacity. The program initially contained a smaller number of benchmarks than Latvia but more than Bulgaria, Hungary and Romania. As the program progressed however, and partly because passage of broad legislation did not necessarily result in actual system reform, confidence declined and the number of conditions mushroomed. As noted in the IMF's staff assessment (IMF, 2013, p. 41) "the blanket legislation to liberalize closed professions was succeeded under the EFF supported program by detailed legislative and regulatory changes on a profession by profession basis." This did not succeed either, as will be discussed below. The point is that the lessons of experience were not followed from the beginning: there should have been fewer conditions and better focused.

The conditionality attached to the program was focused wrongly if the objective was to shift resources to the tradeables sector—especially more exports. Following the 'Washington Consensus' which suggests that factor market imperfections should be addressed before market distortions, several adjustment measures were designed to lower wage costs, in order to help restore competitiveness. It turns out that wage costs were lowered but prices did not fall as much as expected, which resulted in increased poverty. In some instances, the overall price level would actually fall but exports would not rise. Greater efforts probably should have been made earlier on to address product rather than factor market imperfections. However, in my view the problem was deeper: very little attention was paid to the export sector and what it would take to expand Greek exports.

The only serious study on the composition of Greek exports confirms the apparent loss of competitiveness identified by many. It shows that in the period 1996–2006, growth of Greek exports was less than could be expected by the growth of world trade: Greek exports consisted of commodities with less than average growth in world demand and within the group of commodities exported, Greece's share declined (Athanasoglou et al., 2010, p. 19). The study also shows that the long run elasticity of price competitiveness of Greek exports is relatively low "which means that the improvement in export performance through changing export prices requires a rather strong effort" (Athanasoglou et al., 2010, p. 49). Clearly, the internal devaluation was not enough. "There was no way that wage and price reductions could make up for the fact that Greece had a fixed exchange rate" (Michalopoulos, 2017, pp. 250–253).

Recall the composition of Greek exports over the period 2005–2015 discussed earlier. The top five exports in Table 6.3 were petroleum products, aluminum, pharmaceuticals, plastics and machinery of various kinds. As noted earlier, the large petroleum exports reflect the production of several refineries that import crude oil and export refined products. Aluminum exports reflect production of a smelter using bauxite ores and the rest are capital-intensive products: It is not that Greece is not involved in global value chains (see de la Maisonneuve, 2016). It is, but its focus is mostly the capital-intensive part of the chains. The impact of labor costs on the competitiveness of these sectors is decidedly limited.[12]

A great number of the rest of the potential exports depend on agriculture (fruits and vegetables, olive oil, tobacco and cotton (HS52). Anybody who has visited a Greek farm in recent periods would have noticed that most of the labor consists of immigrants (many illegal) from all over the world including Asia, Africa and Albania. Practically all are paid in cash as part of the large grey economy and for them the formal wage sector and what happens to minimum wages, union contracts, etc., is barely relevant. [13] As for cotton, the less said the better: cotton is a product heavy in the use of water, an input in very scarce supply in Greece, making it a product profitable only under very heavy subsidies, which are not appropriate during a period of fiscal stringency.

The main difficulties of expanding exports rested with the administrative procedures and overall business climate and fall under the general rubric of trade facilitation. Weaknesses in trade related institutions is also the main reason for the weak Greek export performance according to a European Commission study (Bowerm et al., 2014). There was practically no discussion of the export sector in any of the lengthy Letters of Intent and MOUs in the early years. No trade expert came from Brussels to help. It was only in the later periods of the EFF that conditionality focused very lightly on these issues, and the customs regulations were improved in 2014 (IMF, 2014). But in 2015 exports fell significantly in part because of the imposition of capital controls and they appear to have declined further in 2016.

"In the second year of the program, the Troika also mishandled the conditionality regarding privatization. Given their uncertainty, proceeds from privatization do not count in filling financial gaps of IMF programs. Yet, the European Commission representative announced publicly a figure of 50 billion euro as a program target without prior consultation with the Greek authorities.[14] The figure is preposterously large especially as it is intended in part to be based on the privatization of Greek public real estate assets which have never been evaluated, not the least because there is no full cadaster of the Greek economy. Whatever the origin, the number created a storm of opposition from all directions, including a number of labor unions. The communist led union of Piraeus Port workers was especially incensed, as the proposals appeared to include fuller privatization of the Piraeus port in which the Chinese company COSCO already had a substantial stake. As a result, we had the oxymoron situation in which a communist led union in a market economy opposed the acquisition of a public asset by a state owned enterprise of a communist country considered even today a non-market economy by the US and the EU. After many years and many false starts, the sale was finalized in early 2017. The strikes however, resulted in significant losses of foreign exchange as for many years they made it impossible for cruise ships to make Piraeus their port of origin or part of their itinerary."

The Greek Government

"Early on and throughout most of the first Stand-By, there was no questioning of the Greek government ownership of the program of fiscal adjustment. Any government that reduces a budget deficit by more than 5% of GDP must have been committed to the program. This was especially the case with the Ministry of Finance and the Prime Minister. While not all aspects of the fiscal reform were implemented on time, as the situation in the Ministry and related agencies was truly chaotic, the bulk of the benchmarks were met. Major problems continued however, with tax evasion.

And as had happened in many developing countries in the 1980s, problems arose with the implementation of the reforms by the other Ministries. The main problems were with privatization and labor reforms. This should not have come as a surprise given that 'socialist' is one of the initials in PASOK, the government party at the time. There were also problems with efforts to open the so-called 'closed professions,' i.e. lawyers, engineers, pharmacists, notaries. There were, and still are, two kinds of issues: either legislation would pass, but the relevant ministries would not implement it; or the 'vested interests' would block its implementation through a variety of means including recourse to the very slow judicial system. To this day and despite various legislative efforts by various governments of the Right, the Left or the Center, Greek pharmacies operate on hours determined by their guild not the relevant legislation and one cannot buy aspirin or other non-prescription drugs anywhere else except in pharmacies.

This kind of ownership problems should not have come as a surprise to the IMF—perhaps the ECB and the Commission were not aware of them because of their lack of experience with these matters, but this issue was central to all the IMF programs in Latin America, Sub-Sahara Africa, everywhere in the 1980s and 1990s. The government meaning the Prime Minister, the Ministry of Finance and the Central Bank would come to an agreement with the IMF (and the World Bank) on a package of reforms that frequently would not be implemented by the rest of the government. And the response should not have been what the IMF did (and to which the government agreed) which is to devise a large number of detailed steps as prior actions, but as the later report states 'ownership could be fostered by focusing on a smaller number of reforms with a clear implementation sequencing' (IMF, 2017). This was written in 2017, regarding actions that took place five years earlier. However, the lessons on these aid issues were clear to the OECD/DAC of twenty years before and the Paris Declaration on Aid Effectiveness in which the IMF participated in the early 2000s. They were ignored by the Troika and the Greek government, both of whom should have known better. Regrettably, the early failures in structural reforms undermined confidence in the government's commitment and resulted in a 'short leash' detailed conditionality later on.

The government also failed in 'selling' the program to the public—partly because the main Ministries involved in the program could only speak about the hardships the program would entail. There were a few voices, arguing that all the measures advocated by the Troika had to be undertaken, irrespective of whether they were part of the onerous "memorandum" because they made sense and would strengthen the Greek economy in the long-run. But these voices were drowned out by the fierce political opposition both by the parties of the Greek Left and those of the Greek Right. There was no consensus for reform in Greece at that time" (Michalopoulos, 2017, pp. 256–258).

Not in the Room

About a year into the first bailout, doubts about its sufficiency started to grow: despite some progress, the 2011 Greek budget deficit continued to be in the range of 10% of GDP and the primary fiscal balance at around −2.5%. Combined with the large decline in GDP, the Debt/GDP ratio deteriorated making the future debt profile unsustainable and a 'debt restructuring became inevitable' (IMF, 2017, p. 8). In the course of the summer of 2011, there was continuing market turmoil, a lot of negotiations in Brussels, discussions with the private sector and a plan for a possible PSI was announced in July 1, 2011.[15] The *Financial Times* wrote that 'the world's largest banks signaled on Friday they were willing to take write-downs on their stocks of Greek debt to help foster a wider solution to the Eurozone debt crisis' (*Financial Times*, 2011).

Following this preliminary announcement there were extensive discussions with the Eurozone Finance Ministers, the Greek government and the ECB. Dallara (2024, p. 162) reports that at that time Trichet told him that "A restructuring of Greek debt would be a mistake." But later that summer of 2011, Trichet noted that while he still had reservations about the Greek restructuring 'with the protections that ECB has received I am prepared to work with you (the IIF) and the governments of Europe to make this a success' (Dallara, 2024, p. 195). Of course, Trichet was right: several weeks before the restructuring (which happened the Spring of 2012), the ECB decided to swap its holding of Greek sovereigns which it had bought at 30% of their value with new Greek bonds which would be excluded from the rescheduling and which the Greek government would have to redeem over time at 100% of their face value. This way the ECB realized a massive profit of more than 18 billion euros. This profit, which ECB has only partially returned to Greece, had been the subject of continuous negotiations in more recent years.

In parallel, there was considerable internal opposition and a government reshuffle in Greece as well as a casual private proposal of the German Minister of Finance Schauble in September that Greece should consider an orderly and supposedly temporary "Grexit" (Papaconstantinou, 2016, p. 328).

All eyes turned to the EU Summit in Cannes scheduled for October 26–27, 2011, in Cannes for a way out of the crisis. The scene is captured by Dallara as follows: "In the midst of market turbulence and political distress, Europe's most senior leaders, the European Commission (EC) and the International Monetary Fund came together with Greece and its private creditors on the night of October 25, 2011 to search for a way out of Greece's monumental debt problem and Europe's crisis" (Dallara, 2024, pp. 17–18).

Remarkably, as the author who was representing the private banking sector later states, when the deal was reached in the early morning of October 26, 2011 "It was quickly noticeable as I glanced about that Greek Prime Minister George Papandreou was nowhere to be seen – he had been left behind in the main meeting room, with all the other Eurozone leaders. I was not surprised by his absence but slightly saddened. It was after all Greece's fate that was being decided" (Dallara, 2024, p. 27).

Some Preliminary Conclusions

The results of the Cannes meeting are discussed in the next chapter. But it is fair to say that to that point, the increased Greek dependence on Europe for both trade and finance failed to produce the desired results in the first decade of its existence.

On trade, the participation in the EMU did little to improve Greek trade performance or increase the proportion of trade directed to EU markets.

On finance, all three major participants in the first Greek bailout failed to heed the lessons of the past. The notion that involvement in a monetary union would inhibit the Greek government from running deficits in violation of the rules in the agreement proved again false—but this time slightly justified by the fact that other members of the agreement also broke the rules—perhaps not by as much—but still with impunity. When the time came to deal with Greek profligacy, the Eurozone partners, not unnaturally, gave priority to saving their own banking system rather than taking the steps that would have helped the longer-term viability of the Greek economy. The IMF, which of course ultimately also reflects the views of governments—sponsored an agreement, which it should have known would not have restored creditworthiness. The agreed macro parameters were bound to produce a decline in incomes much greater than projected, and if the IMF knew, it was constrained by the unwillingness of its major stockholders for putting up more financial assistance or better terms. The result was greater poverty for Greece and a need for further bailouts that would result in the saddling of the Greek economy with a debt whose servicing is causing a major constraint on future growth.

Notes

1. In keeping with Greek traditions characterized by political dynasties, this Karamanlis, was a nephew of the previous leader mentioned in Chapter 4.
2. The third generation scion of another political dynasty.
3. This section and the following two are based in part on Michalopoulos (2017, pp. 241–257).
4. Orphanides called the first bailout the original sin in his 2015 paper. Yet, the bailout contained a lot of sins, not a single one.
5. Tavlas (2019) quotes another Orphanides article "The Euro Area Crisis five years after the Crisis" in *Credit and Capital Markets*, 48, p. 553" in which the above quote by Pohl is linked not to the IMF program but to the establishment of the SMP. Whatever the focus of the quote, it is clear that at that point, neither the German government, nor the ECB gave priority to fixing the Greek economy, but rather to protect the German banks.
6. Baldwin and Giavazzi (2016, p. 35) focuses on the fact excess of domestic investment relative to savings which resulted in the need to borrow foreign capital. But in the case of Greece (and Portugal) the increases in foreign borrowing parallel increases in public sector deficits (p. 35).
7. It also precipitated new IMF support programs in Portugal and Ireland and the establishment of the European Support Mechanism (ESM) in 2012.
8. A number of other countries had attempted to adjust with internal devaluations or with fixed pegs (for example Latvia); but none faced the triple problems affecting Greece.
9. Although the US did provide assistance to Mexico directly.
10. Or, because he wanted to increase the IMF's capitalization or for his own political ambitions as some have claimed (Galbraith, 2016).
11. The West African countries did devalue the West African franc in 1993, the year Trichet left the French Treasury to take over as President of the French Central Bank.

12. The Athanasoglou study says that Greek exports are intensive in the use of 'medium' technology without an explanation of what this means in terms of capital/labor intensity. Yet another study suggests an inverse relationship of Greek exports to unit labor costs (Geronikolaou et al., 2016). The regression analysis on which this conclusion is based is somewhat suspect as it shows a rise in unit labor costs for the period 2004–2009 and a decline for 2009–2014; but Greek exports grew, albeit slowly throughout this period.
13. Loosening labor market legislation, a structural benchmark under the program should have reduced the incentives to hire laborers in the grey market; however the market for agricultural labor was almost wholly outside the formal sector and dominated by immigrants since the fall of the Berlin wall, primarily Albanian and other Eastern European labor, in the early 1990s.
14. One source (Papaconstantinou, 2015) suggests that the number came from the IMF. It may have been used to 'fool' the markets, as debt reduction was still not on the table.
15. Charles Dallara—whom I had met when he was a young assistant to the Assistant Secretary for International Affairs at the US Treasury in the early 1980s, was at the time of the Greek crisis head of the Institute for International Finance. He has written a definitive account of these discussions as well as the subsequent tortuous negotiations with the Eurozone governments, the Greek government and the IMF that ultimately led to a private sector debt reduction scheme (Dallara, 2024).

References

Athanasoglou, P., Backinezos, C., & Georgiou, E. (2010). *Export Performance, Competitiveness and Commodity Composition* (Bank of Greece, Working Paper 114). Bank of Greece.

Baldwin, R., & Giavazzi, F. (Eds.). (2016). *The Eurozone Crisis: A Consensus View of the Causes and a Few Possible Solutions*. CEPR Press. https://cepr.org/publications/books-and-reports/eurozone-crisis-consensus-view-causes-and-few-possible-solutions

Bowerm, U., Mitrou, V., & Ungerer, C. (2014). *The Puzzle of the Missing Greek Exports* (Economic Paper 518). European Commission.

Dallara, C. (2024). *Euroshock*. Rodin Books.

de la Maisonneuve, C. (2016). *How to Boost Export Performance in Greece* (OECD Economic Department Working Paper 1299). OECD.

Dornbush, R. (1996, September/October). Euro Fantasies. *Foreign Affairs*.

Eurostat. (2010). *Report on the EDP Methodological Visits to Greece in 2010*. European Commission, Eurostat.

Financial Times. (2011, July 1). Banks Signal Move on Greek Crisis.

Friedman, M. (1997, August). *The Euro: Monetary Unity to Political Disunity*. Project Syndicat. http://www.projectsyndicat.org/commentary

Galbraith, J. K. (2016). *Welcome to the Poisoned Chalice*. Yale University Press.

Gibson, H., Palivos, T., & Tavlas, G. S. (2014, March). The Crisis in the Euro Area: An Analytic Overview. *Journal of Macroeconomics* (39) B.

Geronicolaou, G., Spyromitrou, E., & Tsintzos, P. (2016). What Drives Greek Exports Performance: A Macrolevel Analysis. In P. E Petrakis (Ed.), *A New Growth Model for the Greek Economy*. Palgrave/Springer.

Gournichas, P., Philippon, T., & Vayanos, D. (2016). *The Analytics of the Greek Crisis* (NBER Macroeconomics Annual #31). MIT Press.

Hardouvelis, G. (2015, July 7). Greece: How to Undo the Damage. *INY Times*.

IEO (Independent Evaluation Office of the IMF). (2016). *The IMF and the Crises in Greece, Ireland and Portugal*. IMF.

IMF. (2013). *Greece: Ex-Post Evaluation of Exceptional Access Under the Stand-By Arrangement* (Country Report No. 13/156). IMF.

IMF. (2014). *Greece: Fifth Review Under the Extended Fund Facility and Request for Waiver of Non-observance of Performance Criterion and Re-phasing of Access* (Staff Report 14/151). IMF.

IMF. (2017). *Greece: Ex Post Evaluation of Exceptional Access Under the 2012 Extended Arrangement* (Country Report 17/44). IMF.

Kathimerini. (2015, June 25). Marathon Discussions in Brussels.

Lazaretou, S. (2021). Greece in the EMU: Economic Benefits and Policy Constraints Lessons Learned and Moving Forward. *Hellenic Review of European Law, International Edition*, 105–134.

Michalopoulos, C. (2017). *Aid, Trade and Development: 50 Years of Globalization*. Palgrave Macmillan.

Orphanides, A. (2015). *The Euro Area Crisis Five Years After the Original Sin* (MIT Sloan Working Paper 5147-15). MIT.

Papaconstantinou, G. (2015, July 9). Re Greece over the Brink. *INY Times*.

Papaconstantinou, G. (2016). *Game Over I Alithia ya tin crisi*. Papadopoulos.

Pisani-Ferry, J. (2014). *The Euro Crisis and Its Aftermath*. Oxford University Press.

Sardelis, C. (2013, March). *Myths and Reality About the Goldman Sachs Issue* (in Greek Μυθοι και Πραγματικοτητα για την υποθεση Goldman Sachs). Οικονομικη Επιθεωρηση.

Stiglitz, J. E. (2015, July 25). Greece, the Sacrificial Lamb. *INY Times*.

Tavlas, G. (2019). *The Theory of Monetary Integration in the Aftermath of the Greek Crisis*. IBL Libri

Wyplosz, C., & Sgherri, S. (2016). *The IMF's Role in Greece in the Context of the 2010 Standby* (IEO Background Paper BP-16/02-11). IMF.

CHAPTER 7

Rescue, Reform and Recovery

Introduction

The Cannes summit resulted in significantly more assistance to Greece from the newly established European Support Mechanism (ESM) and led to a new IMF Extended Fund Facility (EFF) program which however did not calm the markets. The situation improved starting in May 2012 when the newly appointed ECB governor, Mario Draghi[1] uttered the now famous phrase that the ECB will do, 'Whatever it takes' to stabilize the markets and save the euro.

It actually took over four more years, a third IMF program, several Greek elections and new governments to restore stability and growth. This chapter will explore the gory details of the rescue plans and their impact on the Greek economy, society and people. Later chapters will discuss the implications of the Greek story for the future of the Greek economy and the lessons for economic integration efforts more generally.

False Dawn: The Second Bailout[2]

"The Cannes agreement called for the Eurozone countries to provide up to 100 billion euro in new credits on softer terms as well as 30 billion euro for a possible haircut of up to 50% of the private debt. However, this Eurozone agreement was not the end of the story. The Greek Prime Minister, George Papandreou, was deeply concerned that the agreement

C. Michalopoulos, *Greek Foreign Trade and Finance*, Palgrave Studies in Economic History, https://doi.org/10.1007/978-3-031-92104-9_7

would entail significant additional hardship through budget cuts that would involve more reductions on pensions and other areas. He also wanted to show up the opposition, which had opposed the bailout but insisted on wanting to stay in the euro. Thus, he proposed to put the whole agreement up for judgement in a public referendum. Papandreou's referendum proposal resulted in an uproar in the Eurozone, because of its possible implications for the markets and the future of the euro. It also generated opposition within his own party, as a result of which, he agreed to withdraw the referendum proposal as well as resign, to be succeeded by a technocratic government supported by PASOK and New Democracy (ND), the two centrist parties which, with different names, had governed Greece for most of the post-World War II era" (Michalopoulos, 2017, pp. 258–259).

There were many technical aspects of the proposed haircut that had to be sorted-out and a lot of unhelpful suggestions from Germany and other Eurozone members that had to be addressed. Dallara (2024, p. 333) reports that a proposal emerged from the German government that "Given the disappointing compliance so far, Greece has to accept shifting budgetary sovereignty to the European level for a certain period of time." This was not any different from the reestablishment of the International Financial Audit Commission a little more than a century later.

It fell upon the technocratic government of headed by Loukas Papademos, a former governor of the Bank of Greece and deputy Governor of the ECB to pass the legislation needed as prior actions for the second bailout amid extraordinary demonstrations supported by the opposition Left and Right parties. I happened to be in Greece that fateful evening in mid-February 2012 and wrote a letter to a number of friends and relatives from which I quote:

> I just came back from Athens, where at midnight, last Sunday (February 12), I witnessed live on TV what constituted possibly the next to the last act of the modern Greek tragedy: the Greek parliament voting in the affirmative, with a large majority to accept the onerous terms of the latest bailout, while on a split screen one could see several buildings burning and the police battling thousands of hooded anarchists who were throwing Molotov cocktails.
>
> Sunday's events resulted in two sets of ruins: First, a number of buildings were destroyed including two movie theaters and one restaurant, whose charred ruins I visited with sadness on Monday amidst residual tear gas fumes; these will be rebuilt. What will not be rebuilt is the second set of

ruins, which consists of the Greek political party system, which (with the exception for the few years of the nasty colonels) has governed Greece for the last sixty years. After the vote, almost 50 MPs from the two ruling parties (PASOK and ND) which have been supporting the government, have been expelled from their parties for not voting for the bailout. PASOK is in total disarray and may not muster 10% of the vote in the next elections. The decline of the two parties may not be a bad thing in the long run: they have been responsible for the patronage and corruption that has been endemic in Greek governments. But in the short run, it will force the creation of multi-party governments requiring the building of consensus for any policy action-something that Greek parties have not done for years. And it will make staying the course in implementing the commitments of the new memorandum even more difficult, possibly heading into a more tragic finale.

There are no big time heroes in this play. The only heroes I can think of are the thousands of pensioners who will have to eke out an existence with as little as 250 euros a month or less; or perhaps the shopkeeper near Syntagma in central Athens whose shop had been vandalized by anarchists on two previous occasions and who on Sunday night crashed a bat on the head of an anarchist forcing him and his buddies to scamper.

There are many villains. On the Greek side, I will start with the tax authorities and personnel, the bulk of whom are either incompetent or corrupt. As of the end of the last fiscal year, the Greek government was apparently owed 8 billion euros in taxes and fines from roughly 25,000 individuals or companies; it had been able to collect only 100 million. If it had collected a bit more than half of the total, it would have had no budget deficit. A second collective villain is the thousands of doctors, lawyers, plumbers, electricians and many other members of the so called 'liberal' professions who habitually report only about one tenth of their taxable income. A third collective villain is the so called 'syndicalists' the trade union people whom the Greeks in a play of words call the syndicate robbers...

Competitiveness cannot increase in the short run by opening up the professions; and as inflation is low and the exchange rate fixed there is little one can do...Alas, the economy under the best of circumstances will be in a depressed state for years to come.

What is needed is for the creditors to find a way to be more generous; also, what is needed is for a new Greek government to manage to behave more responsibly for a sufficient period to also ease the uncertainty. This is almost like asking for a *deus ex machina* who used to resolve problems in ancient tragedies. I end on an optimistic note, not because I believe in miraculous interventions. Rather I believe in Greek ingenuity and, unlike what one hears in Northern Europe these days, Greek industriousness and

> work ethic. Most Greeks work hard in order to consume more and they invest a lot in the education of their children. So that even if there is a disorderly default, a few years later the economy will pick up within the euro, if there is still a euro, or with the drachma a currency whose history is much longer than the euro. (Michalopoulos, 2012)

"The PSI haircut took another month or so to be agreed and resulted in a 53% reduction of the private debt. However, as a great deal of the foreign bond holders had already dumped their bonds, the haircut fell disproportionately on the Greek (and Cypriot banks) which had to be recapitalized as well as on Greek pension funds. At the same time, there was continuous loss of bank deposits. The Greek banking system, which, unlike the Irish banks had not been overextended at the start of the problem, became shakier and shakier" (Michalopoulos, 2017, p. 260).

A new EFF agreement was requested and obtained from the IMF of 28 billion euro with a set of conditionalities involving "rapid fiscal and external adjustment to be accompanied by politically difficult structural reforms in support of the (authorities) strong preference to remain in the euro area" (IMF, 2017, p. 11). The IMF staff felt that it would have been desirable to have a slower but longer adjustment period, but were willing to give the Greek authorities a chance to implement the program recognizing that "the new program is a bold step in the right direction but given the challenges and the track record is subject to exceptional risks" (IMF, 2012).

"The IMF staff report contained two 'boxes' one of which essentially said that internal devaluation was extremely difficult and rarely, if ever, succeeded. There is little to disagree with this judgement, especially as contrary to expectations, the internal devaluation would have had to take place in an overall deflationary international environment requiring actual declines in nominal wages and prices, a very difficult feat indeed. The other box said that leaving the euro would result in many unpleasant and unquantifiable adverse repercussions for the economy (IMF, 2012). Thus, the IMF staff protected itself on paper against any program outcome. It is hard to fault them: the only alternative was even more financing from the Eurozone. That was not forthcoming. While it is correct to argue that Eurozone financing was self-serving to a considerable extent, it is also important to consider that some of this financing had to come from Eurozone countries that were significantly poorer than Greece. In addition, it is true that, because Greeks had to cope with inflation for so long, they channeled their savings into real estate. As a result, although their per capita income was less than the Eurozone average, real assets were significantly higher, leading to significant political opposition to the Greek bailouts by the general public in Western Europe.

After two parliamentary elections, a new coalition government was established headed by ND but including PASOK and DHMAR a smaller left wing party. The new government started to implement the EFF program with considerable success for almost two years. It had the benefit of the new ECB boss, Mario Draghi, whose now famous dictum in May of 2012 that the ECB will do 'whatever it takes' to support the euro resulted in no more 'Grexit' discussions for a while. In November, there was a softening of the terms of the Eurozone official loans and a return to Greece of some of the ECB profits on the Greek bonds.

There was long a list of conditionalities, 44 prior actions plus 43 structural benchmarks, of which ten were converted into prior actions—compared to 9 prior actions in the Cyprus program, 5 in the case of Ireland and 17 in Portugal (IMF, 2017, Fig. 21, p. 28). The conditionalities contained the usual efforts to improve fiscal and general government performance, the labor market, opening up the professions etc. and for the first time paid attention to trade issues (see Chapter 6). Perhaps its greatest accomplishment was the introduction of a new unified tax on real estate (Michalopoulos, 2017, pp. 261–262).

In the course of 2012, and most importantly in November and December of that year, additional steps were taken to amend the original terms of the loans given to Greece in 2010 under the so-called Greek Loan Facility from ten years to 30 years with a grace period of 10 years and lower interest rates. Moreover, it was agreed to lengthen the grace and repayment periods of the EFSF loan, granted earlier in the year, to 10 years and 32.5 years respectively. These adjustments resulted in the loans being converted from essentially commercial terms for the original 'Greek Facility' loan and the EFSF to concessional loans which contained a 'grant element' of 37% in the former and 61% in the latter (Schumacher & Weder-di Mauro, 2015, p. 296).[3]

"Performance was not perfect but until mid-2014, it appeared to be slightly better than under the stand-by, partly because there seemed to be greater ownership of the program by the governing coalition. The review by the Troika in May 2014 said, "To have reached a surplus on primary fiscal and current account balances so swiftly is an extraordinary adjustment by any international comparison" (IMF, 2014, p. 4). The government was on track to achieve a primary surplus of 1.5% and the "Fiscal Adjustment continues to impress" (IMF, 2014, p. 22). In the spring, the government managed to return to the markets for the first time in four years with a five and half year bond for 3 billion euro at 4.95%. The GDP growth was projected to be positive and it looked finally like a turning point had been reached.

Unfortunately then, politics 'interfered.' SYRIZA, the main opposition party following the two elections, continued its hard opposition against the program and reform fatigue appeared to have set in. It was expressed in losses for the ruling coalition in the European elections in June. In the summer of 2014, the government took two steps that weakened its position. The first was that it forced the resignation of H. Theoharis, the Director General for Revenue, a technocrat professional, highly respected by the Troika. The other was the sudden closing down of the public television stations in order to meet its commitment for government personnel reductions. The latter action resulted in another round of massive demonstrations and the departure of the DHMAR party from the government coalition.

In the fall, S&P and Moody's upgraded Greek bonds and the banking system had started to accumulate deposits. The European program of support was ending and there was a question of what, if anything, would replace it, while the IMF EFF was to last until 2016. The government would have preferred to have no program at all, but probably would have agreed to a contingent credit. In retrospect, it appears that during this period the government also started to loosen the budgetary strings. A scheduled Troika visit for the fall was repeatedly postponed as it appeared that the country was headed for elections: the President's term was coming to an end and a replacement had to be approved by a majority of at least 180 MPs, a number that the government was unable to secure. In the absence of agreement on a new President, the constitution required new parliamentary elections.

The New Democracy government had been campaigning on a platform that Greece no longer needed external support from the IMF or anybody, the hated 'memorandum' would be torn up and Greece would be able to tap the markets on its own. Given this position, the last thing the government needed was a Troika mission that would have discovered that the bulk of the structural reforms were not being put in place, that the target of a primary surplus of 1.5% GDP would not be achieved and that significant budget stringency would continue. In the event, the overall deficit for 2014 was about 4% of GDP and the primary surplus close to zero-good results but probably not sufficient to guarantee that Greece could borrow from the markets the large amounts that it needed in 2015.

We will never know. Prime Minister Samaras came to Washington in November 2014 to plead his case but got no takers from the IMF who thought that he will lose the election and did not wish to be bound vis a vis the new government. It is reported that at the December 2014 Eurogroup meeting, the Commission sided with the Greek government that it had done enough to receive the next installment of funding, but the IMF and the ECB objected (Hardoubelis, 2015). As a result, the European program was extended to the end of February 2015 but no money was released" (Michalopoulos, 2017, pp. 262–263).

"The end result was that fiscal and debt sustainability, as crucial as they were, put far too much pressure on social and political- one might say democratic sustainability" (Dallara, 2024, p. 393). SYRIZA won the January 2015 election, formed a coalition with ANEL, (a right wing party whose main interest was in securing the Ministry of Defense for its leader) and ushered a new adventure for the Greek economy and people.

A Left Turn to a Dead End

The acronym of SYRIZA in Greek means Coalition of the Radical Left. It was headed at the time by Alexis Tsipras, a young and charismatic leader and included a number of left leaning groups including splinters of the communist party. For years, it had argued about the unfairness of the 'memoranda' and the burdens they imposed on the Greek people. Soon after it won the election, the government had to face urgent negotiations with the dreaded Troika about extending the European program of support that was to end in February 2015. But before it did that, it announced a number of steps which helped set a tone for the upcoming discussions: all the civil servants fired with the closing of the public television stations by the previous government would be rehired,[5] and the Troika was no longer welcome in Athens. Only technical teams were welcome. The political, i.e. Minister-level negotiations with '*the institutions*' would take place in Brussels.

The government publicly stated that it was in agreement with 70% of the memorandum conditionality—for example, that which related to reducing tax evasion and strengthened governance and administration. There were four major issues: The debt, and the related macro framework, the issue of pensions, the labor market legislation and privatization (Galbraith, 2016, pp. 12–13). They were correct on the first—the prospective macro framework continued to be too restrictive because of the debt and not likely to result in restoration of growth in the near future; partially correct on pensions, and ideologically driven and hence mostly incorrect on the question of labor markets and privatization.

The macro framework continued to call for a substantial primary surplus aiming to reduce the size of the official debt, which would have undoubtedly resulted in continued GDP stagnation. It could only have been achieved in part by further reducing pensions. These had already been reduced substantially but still accounted for a significant portion of the budget, because earlier retirements and firing of civil servants under previous administrations had increased their rolls; and the finances of the pension funds had been hurt by the debt haircut. And all this without any desire by the Eurozone, for political reasons, to even consider a reduction of the official debt burden.

The government's position on the labor front and privatization was less solid. There was little reason to believe that reversing the loosening up of the labor market done by the previous governments would have raised incomes for the really poor. While it was correct that privatization should not lead to 'fire sales,' irrespective of the nuanced government position, statements and actions by various government officials continuously undermined the government's ownership of the program.

The February discussions were artful in papering over temporarily the disagreements. They resulted in kicking the bucket down the road somewhat, as the program was extended until June 30, 2015. In the meantime, discussions were to take place to reach agreement, but no money was released in the absence of a Troika assessment. The government did not want the latter, because it would have shown the increased deficit caused by its increased spending linked to the new hires as well as a reduction in budget revenues. The discussions were taking place under the Damoclean sword of the ECB's possible cutting off credit to the Greek commercial banks, and continuing uncertainty about the government's ability to meet external payments either of which would have meant unruly Greek default.

Yannis Varoufakis, the Greek Minister of Finance during this period has written an extensive memoire of these negotiations (Varoufakis, 2017). In the memoire, he maintains that he was committed to keep Greece in the Eurozone, provided he would be able to reach a reasonable agreement on reducing Greek debt with its Eurozone creditors. This was critical to loosening the requirement for maintaining a large primary fiscal deficit of 3.5% to 4%, which in turn was an essential condition for restoring growth.

He was also concerned about the progressive hemorrhaging of bank deposits that he blamed in large part to the lack of cooperation of the Greek Central Bank. In fact, the decline in deposits began *pari- passu* with the increased popularity of Tsipras and SYRIZA's statements based on the party platform which Varoufakis himself characterized "incoherent" as "it promised wage rises benefits and investment paid for with resources of funding which were imaginary or illegal" (Varoufakis, 2017, p. 88).[6] Varoufakis was convinced that he had a potential weapon in threatening the ECB with a loss on the Greek bonds held by the latter. In parallel, he ordered the secret elaboration of a plan for Grexit in case he was not able to reach agreement in reducing the debt and the ECB stopped completely the emergency liquidity it was providing to the Greek banking system.

Schauble, the German Finance Minister, strongly opposed any talk about debt relief. He fundamentally wanted Greece out of the Eurozone because he did not trust any Greek government's commitments, and if Greece were to stay in the Eurozone, it would have to follow *his* rules, which required continued fiscal austerity, which he knew was not likely to produce any growth. Schauble was supported in all this by a number of other governments, the Netherlands, Finland and several Eastern European countries as well as Spain that had also faced difficulties and did not want to give Greece an easy ride. The European Commission was more supportive of the Greek position, but typically less powerful in the actual Eurozone negotiations. The IMF wanted to ensure that any new program would have restored debt sustainability.

Varoufakis' approach alienated his Eurozone partners, introduced doubts in his own party and contributed to a frigid relationship with the Greek Central Bank. Characteristically, Tsipras ordered Varoufakis to tell the IMF Managing Director, Christine Lagarde that Greece will default on an IMF payment in May although he had decided not to. In fact, the Greek government made the payment using some of its SDRs.[7]

In May, Tsipras sidelined Varoufakis from the negotiations, which continued in Brussels. In the meantime, given the increasing uncertainties, bank deposits declined as did investment, for who in their right mind would consider investing in the Greek economy under such circumstances?

Varoufakis says little about the problems introduced by the 'internal devaluation' and for the need for essential structural reforms. Yet, he was right on the need to reduce the debt, and the related fiscal austerity. On this issue, he received the support of a large number of distinguished economists worldwide. Unfortunately, he did not know the difference between being right and getting it right or getting others to agree.[8]

I arrived in Greece for my annual vacation in early June carrying with me a substantial amount of currency in US dollars and euros for our expenses, as I feared a banking system collapse. I regret that I was not wrong. Final discussions on a program were going on in Brussels in the last week of June. The Greek side put together a proposal but the *institutions* came back with a text full of changes. The differences were extensive but focused on excruciating details: should the increase in the upper range of the VAT include hotels or not? Should all businesses be asked to prepay their income taxes as the creditors wanted or should business with profits over 500,000 euros pay an extra tax, etc. (*Kathimerini*, June 27, 2015). They showed how little confidence the creditors had in the government and how not to put together a rescue program. Tsipras canceled further discussions and returned to Athens. I predicted there would be a run on the banks.

Tsipras announced a referendum on the institutions' proposals early Saturday June 27. The referendum was vaguely drafted and ill construed. Some said it was unconstitutional. The government recommended a NO vote hoping that this would strengthen its negotiating ability. The ballot itself had a NO vote as the first option—a telling point. A YES vote was supposed to be supportive of the *institutions*. Some interpreted a YES vote to mean staying in the Eurozone and NO a vote to leave. There was a run on the banks over the weekend and the Bank of Greece closed the banks on Monday morning June 29. Famous liberal economists like Krugman wrote in support of NO (*INYT Times*, June 30, 2015).

I voted YES and lost as the NO votes carried the day by a large margin, 61% to 39%. Then something funny happened. For the first time, Tsipras asked for support from the opposition parties to negotiate a deal that would permit Greece to stay in the Eurozone. Varoufakis, the Finance Minister who had contemplated an exit from the euro and alienated a lot of his colleagues in Europe in six months of futile negotiations resigned, saying cheekily in his blog: "soon after the announcement of the referendum results, I was made aware of certain preference by some European participants and assorted partners for my absence from its meetings; an idea that the Prime Minister judged to be potentially helpful to him in reaching an agreement" (*Kathimerini*, June 27, 2015). In his book, he states that he was asked to stay with the government but in a different job, so he decided to resign. As Papaconstantinou has made famous, the game was truly over (Papaconstantinou, 2016).

Armed with the support of the other political parties and a new Finance Minister, Tsipras went to Brussels to 'negotiate' with the Eurozone leaders the weekend of July 11–12. The road had reached a dead end and beyond it lay the cliff of Grexit. He was presented with two alternatives: either leave the Eurozone for five years according to a proposal circulated by the German government or agree to the demands of the Eurozone leaders regarding reforms and even greater austerity. As to the needed debt reduction, he was given only vague promises that it may be discussed in the future provided Greece made sufficient progress in the agreed reform package that included all the things the government had opposed earlier including the establishment of a new agency to handle privatization and government asset management" (Michalopoulos, 2017, pp. 264–268).

Given these 'options' Tsipras turned around and a new 'memorandum' was soon to emerge.[9] "After five years of deep economic and social pain, in the beginning of 2015 the economy was growing again and the Greek state was spending less than it collected in taxes (aside from interest payments). What lay ahead was a promise of additional debt relief and economic and social recovery…It took five short months to destroy all this. A projected 2.5% growth rate for this year turned into a recession and the primary surplus turned into a deficit—all courtesy of the SYRIZA-ANEL government under Prime Minister Alexis Tsipras" (Papaconstantinou, *INY Times*, July 9, 2015).[10]

In addition, of course, the banking system was ruined. While the banks re-opened, capital controls continued, with adverse repercussions for all business activity and especially investment and exports. At the end of the day, Greece had a larger debt burden than which it had started. To top it all, during this summer of discontent, there was a mass influx of refugees from Syria and elsewhere through Turkiye, further challenging the government's capacity to operate.

The government received relief through a bridge credit that permitted it to meet its obligations to the IMF whose repayment had been delayed. It then obtained a new credit from the European Stability Mechanism of 86 million euro on softer terms than previously. The austerity measures imposed were much harsher than had been offered by the Eurozone earlier in the spring, partly because in the meantime the economy and the budget accounts had deteriorated. The long-term problem persisted. As Stiglitz wrote "The Germans say there is to be no debt write-off and that the IMF must be part of the program. But the IMF cannot participate in a program in which debt levels are unsustainable, and Greece's debts are unsustainable" (*INY Times*, Stiglitz July 27, 2015). In the end, the IMF agreed to participate in the ongoing reviews but did not provide any new funding. After six months of useless acrimonious negotiations and a government 'program' that scared investors, domestic and foreign, Greece was in worse shape than a year earlier.

Tsipras, facing a revolt from SYRIZA's extreme left over the Eurozone agreement, resigned and called for new elections in September of 2015. SYRIZA won the elections, with a slightly smaller majority but was still able to form a new government in a coalition, again with ANEL. The government started implementing the third memorandum that contained a number of important reforms, for example in unifying the various pension funds. Much to its chagrin, it had to participate in discussions with *four* institutions, as representatives of the ESM had been added to the troika making it the *quartet*, and the latter no longer met with the government in Brussels, but usually in Athens.

Stability and Stagnation

The second Tsipras government had two main achievements: (a) It sustained the fiscal austerity demanded by the Troika as the government primary budget continued to be in surplus more or less on target for the next four years—but at great costs to the Greek economy. (b) At the insistence of the creditors, it finalized a number of changes in social benefits and contributions that helped reduce income inequality between 2014 and 2019: 37–40% of the fall in inequality (during this period) was due to such policy changes,[11] with most of the decline due to the changes in benefits (Matsaganis et al., 2024).

The government's ownership of other parts of the structural adjustment program, in particular privatization, was conspicuously lacking. In the summer of 2016, the agreement with COSCO for the privatization of the Pireaus port was submitted to the Parliament for final approval. At the last minute and without consulting with the Chinese firm, the Minister in charge introduced certain changes detrimental to the firm.

The timing was extremely unfortunate, as that very day Tsipras was about to meet with the top of China's government in a formal visit to Beijing. Following the Chinese firm's loud protests, the changes were withdrawn and the legislation passed.[12]

In June 2017, there was a new and spectacular dose of muddling through and kicking the bucket down the road. Following the passage of legislation by the Greek parliament for the implementation of a number of agreed conditions under the program, the Euro group agreed to provide the Greek government with 8.5 billion euro, bringing the total amount disbursed so far to around 40 billion euro out of 80 billion approved in 2015.

The Greek government committed itself to maintain a 3.5% primary budget surplus until 2022 and a 2% surplus for decades thereafter. The IMF continued to believe that the Greek debt is unsustainable without further easing of its burden by the Eurozone creditors. However, the Eurozone creditors refused to commit to an easing of the debt burden until the completion of the program in 2018. They indicated a willingness to consider at that point a further extension of loan maturities between 0 and 15 years as well as the possibility of tying future debt repayments to growth performance. On its part, the IMF also committed itself to consider the possibility of a $2 billion standby, when the debt burden was judged to be sustainable. The Eurozone governments also agreed to help with additional investment funds as well as to assist the Greek government reenter the capital markets at the end of the program in 2018. In the meantime, there were supposed to be four more reviews as well as another 10 billion or so disbursed under the program.

I wrote at the time that "The agreement reflects two facts: the lack of confidence of the Eurozone creditors in the commitment of the Greek government to implement sound economic policies and the politicization of the Eurozone assistance program. Both are bad omens for the future and unless changes are made, they are likely to result in continued stagnation of the Greek economy and suffering for the Greek people" (Michalopoulos, 2017, p. 270).

To that point, the most striking statistic of the crisis of the previous eight years was not the decline in GDP of 25% but the spectacular decline in investment—both public and private. By contrast, consumption fell less, since households used up their savings. The small increase in GDP in 2016 was fueled by an increase in consumption, as Greeks continued to reduce their savings. At 75%, the decline in investment was the largest by far of all the countries that suffered the kind of original shocks that Greece suffered. How could labor productivity grow under these circumstances?

Eurozone assistance to investment had increased considerably in the 2013–2015 period, but had fallen off drastically in 2016–2018 (see Table 6.3). The 2017 commitment to increase Eurozone help on investment did not result in significant additional flows until 2019—partly due to the ineffectiveness of the Greek government investment agency.

The deal with the Eurozone partners committing Greece to maintain a 3.5% primary budget surplus meant continued fiscal stringency until 2022. At a time when the euro had strengthened, further internal devaluation was necessary to maintain exports. All this amounted to a lack of stimulus to the economy. The budget constraint led to the establishment of an equilibrium at low levels of capacity utilization with no growth and a vicious circle. Incomes were growing very slowly, if at all; as a result, government revenues stagnated, the debt had to be repaid and the only way to do this, given large expenditures on defense[13] was to squeeze expenditures, resulting in stagnant incomes and so on. Pensions and investment had borne the bulk of the budget cuts. Pensions could not be squeezed much further without causing further social unrest.

"There has also been an extensive malfunction of institutions that further slowed growth and undermined economic recovery. Greece appears as a country simultaneously experiencing the most severe recession after the global crisis and the most pronounced fall in all World Bank Governance Indicators. The crumbling of institutions accelerated at the advent of the crisis. It may partly explain the inability of the consolidation programs to implement reforms and speed the exit from recession" (Christodoulakis, 2019, p. 27).

A new debt deal was obviously needed. 2017 was not the best time to organize such a deal; if there was ever a good time, given the sin of converting private sector obligations into public debt under the earlier bailouts. Europeans were starting to breathe a sigh of relief that the populist storm had been weathered and pro-European sentiment was on the rise in Greece. Yet, there were still uncertainties down the road. A deal on the debt could not be done before the German elections in September 2017. There was also a fatigue of having to deal with continued extended negotiations with the Greek government and politicization leading to pettiness: Spain thought about attaching as a condition to participating in the Greek bailout that the Greek government agreed to pay the legal fees of a Spanish consultant who was unfairly accused of some misdeed and was facing a day in a Greek court (Michalopoulos, 2017, p. 272).

GDP grew at a rate of 1.4% in 2017. In late July 2018, the IMF announced that even if the projected reforms were accomplished, debt would be sustainable in the medium term but not in the long run (IMF, July 2018; Michalopoulos, 2018). There was another review of the program in late 2018 in anticipation of terminating the program at the end of the year. The European Commission found that while the government achieved the 3.5% targeted primary surplus, it did so by accumulating arrears. There were increases in government employment, the usual delays in privatization and in the passage of several pieces of legislation (Michalopoulos, 2019). Nevertheless, at the end of 2018, the earlier extensions of the grace periods and repayments for the Greek facility loans were confirmed and the ESFS loan maturities extended to 2070. Still some analysts were skeptics: The Peterson Institute noted in an article on the Greek debt that no country had ever run a primary fiscal surplus of 2% for forty years as called by that agreement and a new Greek debt crisis was around the corner (https://www.piie.com/microsites/greek-debt-crisis-no-easy-way-out). The Peterson Institute was wrong on an impending debt crisis. Yet, the road ahead contained huge challenges.

It took another year of anemic 1.7% growth in 2018, the year-end finding Greece with incomes 20% less than at 2012, the year of 'whatever it takes' and unemployment at 19.3% compared with 27.3%. The balance of payments on current account was −3.0% of GDP compared to −10%of GDP and the debt/GDP ratio at 191%. A lot of the cost of the adjustment fell on wage earners as the labor unions resisted labor market reforms. The Commission report looking ahead was not optimistic: "Overall the balance of risks is tilted to the downside" (Michalopoulos, 2019). So what can be made of the benefits of EU membership in light of this outcome?

The Benefits and Challenges of Economic Dependence—A Second Look

It is quite clear that after the failure of the first bailout, the Eurozone partners helped Greece enormously—partly to compensate for their earlier less generous efforts. The IMF also helped, but there was no way that Greece could have found elsewhere the billions of euros in loans that the Eurozone provided. Similarly, the Eurozone continued to provide a considerable amount of grants through various programs—that averaged net about 2.5% of GDP and 12% of investment for the period 2013–2018. I suspect these considerations and others, more political in nature, weighed heavily on Tsipras when he made the famous somersault and decided to negotiate the third bailout.

However, the assistance came in a form that created challenges, the main of which was saddling the Greek economy with large amounts of official debt that required very tight budgetary policies for decades. "The 2012 debt restructuring came late at the cost of heavier and self-defeating fiscal austerity. An unprepared, asymmetric European Monetary Union (EMU) raised the cost of crisis management. In many ways, the Greek crisis paved the way for the reforms in the EMU" (Pagoulatos, 2020, p. 22). The crisis precipitated the establishment of the EMS; the recognition that a debt restructuring should accompany a drawing form the EMS, became a rule in 2018. The process seems to confirm the view of many that the EU moves forward toward greater integration, only under crises conditions.

There was also another related challenge that was not addressed then and is still a problem today. The monetary union had rules regarding the fiscal deficit, but there were no rules regarding the degree of adjustment in the balance of payments among various countries in the group. The Greek crisis may have had its origin in the large budgetary deficits and expansion of credit in the early 2000s, but was precipitated by a balance of payments deficit. This is the same issue that came up in the discussion of the functioning of the Latin Monetary Union in (Chapter 2).

Some years back I wrote: "In the last decade, countries in the periphery, Greece, Italy, Ireland, Portugal and Spain have all reduced their current account deficits as a percent of GDP—some have turned them into surpluses (see Table 7.1). By contrast, Germany has increased its current account *surplus* from 4.6% of GDP in 2005 to 8.4% in 2015. That year, while Greece was struggling mightily to achieve an internal devaluation, Germany through its own macroeconomic policies achieved a further *undervaluation* of its real exchange rate by 10–20% compared to 5–15% in 2014 (IMF, 2016, p. 7).

It is not new that surplus countries like to throw all the adjustment onto the shoulders of deficit countries. In 1960–1961, there were serious imbalances in international payments under the then prevailing system of fixed exchange rates. The group of surplus countries included the usual suspects: Germany, the Netherlands, Japan and some other Europeans.

Table 7.1 Current account balance as % of GDP for selected countries

Country	*2000*	*2005*	*2008*	*2009*	*2010*	*2012*	*2014*	*2015*
Greece	−7.5	−7.4	−14.5	−10.9	−10.1	−2.5	−1.6	0.1
Ireland	–	−3.4	−5.6	−2.1	1.0	4.1	3.5	10.2
Italy	−0.5	−1.6	−2.8	−1.8	−3.4	−0.4	1.8	1.6
Portugal	−10.9	−9.9	−12.2	−10.4	−10.2	−1.8	0.0	0.4
Spain	−4.4	−7.5	−9.3	−4.3	−3.9	−0.3	1.0	1.4
Average	−5.8	−6.0	−8.9	−5.9	−5.3	−0.2	1.0	2.7
Germany	−1.7	4.6	5.6	5.8	5.6	7.0	7.3	8.4

Source IMF

On the opposite side were not weaklings like Greece and Portugal but the US. The latter demanded and Germany and the Netherlands agreed to revalue their currencies upward by about 5% in February 1961. "What is necessary at this time is to have the surplus countries take further steps to make the exchange rate adjustments effective in stimulating their imports and restraining their exports. For this purpose, the surplus countries must lower interest rates to expand home demand…" (Bernstein, 1961, p. 83). They did not expand demand; but they did revalue, and soon the dollar also had to float.

Exchange rates are fixed and monetary policy does not vary within the currency union. The only thing that works is a more expansive fiscal policy for surplus countries. The IMF staff report on Germany for 2016 (IMF, 2016, p. 10) cautiously states: "a looser fiscal position than currently envisaged through 2016–2021 would be appropriate. This would also modestly reduce the current account gap (surplus)." Unless Germany and the other surplus countries are prepared to adjust their policies to some degree the euro will not survive and/or some countries including Greece will leave it as their continued participation will demand indefinite stagnation. And if they leave the euro, they are not going to pay back the German taxpayers" (Michalopoulos, 2017, pp. 273–275).

Others agree: "The Greek experience amply demonstrated the asymmetric Euro Area treatment of what was to a significant extent a systemic crisis of an asymmetric monetary union. Adjustment was overwhelmingly confined to the borrower countries, without a sufficient EMU response or countervailing stimulus on the part of creditor economies. As crisis countries were sharply reducing their deficits through fiscal austerity and internal devaluation, an offsetting stimulus was missing" (Pagoulatos, 2020, p. 15). The problem remains.

A similar view was recently expressed in an article by D. Katsikas (2024, p. 22). "The Greek crisis is the result of a "mutual failure" on the European and domestic fronts. On the one hand, the economic governance agreed upon at Maastricht was clearly inadequate to support the operation of a monetary union comprising many widely diverse economies; on the other hand, given EMU's economic and institutional architecture, Greece was clearly ill-prepared and unwilling to undertake the necessary adjustments to survive in the Eurozone. The mishandling of the crisis by the EMU member states and institutions was unsurprising. Northern Europe's member states, led by Germany, were not prepared to share in the cost of adjustment or to agree to new supranational institutions that could alleviate part of it. Given the design failures in the MoUs and the weaknesses of the Greek political economy, the result was an unnecessarily deep and prolonged crisis, which devastated the Greek economy and led to political instability."

There is still another issue raised extensively at the time: were the challenges and costs associated with the staying the currency union worth it? At the time, the discussion had focused on Grexit—not Brexit. The latter is definitely different, as the UK was not a member of the currency union and not at all a country in the periphery.

I wrote in 2017 "Eurozone exits had not been contemplated at its establishment but the European community has always been able to devise legal approaches to achieve commonly desired results. As long as Greece continues its membership in the European Union an exit from the euro is manageable. The details of reintroducing the drachma have been discussed elsewhere and need be repeated here (Amiel & Hyppolite, 2016). There will be a need to maintain tight fiscal and monetary policy to curb inflation and capital controls for the new currency to settle at a new exchange rate. GDP will drop again and the poor will suffer the most. Official reserves of the Bank of Greece stand around US$6 billion, less than two months of imports. They would need to be augmented through support from the IMF which has done this many times before. The whole process will be painful and it would be a shame if it were to happen; but it will happen at some point unless the debt burden is substantially reduced, macroeconomic policy is loosened and growth returns. The social costs of maintaining the current muddling through cannot be tolerated indefinitely" (Michalopoulos, 2017, p. 275).[14]

I still believe that staying in the euro was the right choice at the time, around 2015, when Varoufakis and others had been contemplating an exit. I now think that, if anything, Greece may have been better off had it threatened to walk out of the currency union, much earlier, in 2010, and pushed for a private sector haircut then. It may have been able to avoid the long declines in economic activity that stretched for years. It did not, essentially for political reasons. There is no point in trying to rewrite that history now.

The last part of my 2017 comments is as valid today as it was then. "The currency union must be strengthened and Greek government policy must improve." Fortunately there is hope that both may materialize. The European project has been strengthened and Greek economic policy has improved.

Notes

1. I had met Draghi thirty years earlier when he was a young, energetic and highly competent Executive Director for Italy and Greece at the World Bank.
2. This and the next section of this chapter are taken with minor editorial changes from Michalopoulos (2017, pp. 258–269).
3. Lazaretou (2021, p. 10) notes however, that while these agreements were made at the end of 2012, they were not actually implemented until the end 2018 (see Chapter 8).
4. The main Greek communist party KKE continued to obtain around 5–10% of the votes but stayed in opposition.
5. As well as the cleaning ladies of the Ministry of Finance who had also been fired.
6. An excerpt from a speech by the Governor of the Bank of Greece quoted by Varoufakis (2017, p. 106) was not helpful in dealing with the problem, but I am not familiar with the rest of the speech or the context.
7. Varoufakis says that the Governor of the Greek Central Bank called him to say that "650 million euro had miraculously been discovered idling around in some forgotten account that happened to be stuffed with funds that we were allowed to use to repay the IMF" (Varoufakis, 2017, pp. 406–407). In fact these funds constituted part of Greece's official foreign exchange reserves, whose existence is regularly reported by the Bank on a monthly basis.

8. This is a Dutch proverb: 'Het verschil tussen gelijk hebben en gelijk krijgen'.
9. Tsoukalis (2023, p. 94) states that Tsipras' somersault got an assist from Draghi who threatened him with withholding liquidity from the Greek banks—another dimension of 'whatever it takes.'
10. Varoufakis claims that the economy was still declining when SYRIZA took over, based on a four month moving average of quarterly GNI (Varoufakis, 2017, p.126). The facts are: GDP growth in constant prices was −3.24% in 2013, +0.35% in 2014 and −0.22% in 2015 (World Bank, 2017).
11. 'The introduction of guaranteed minimum income took place against the indifference or active opposition of key domestic actors; external actors (the EU, the IMF, the World Bank) played a key role in arguing for guaranteed minimum income, imposing legislative changes to make it happen, and providing technical assistance to the Greek government and public administr*ation*' (Matsaganis, 2018, p. 1).
12. One wonders the wisdom of selling as opposed to leasing the country's biggest port.
13. Other than the US, Greece has been for many years and still is the NATO country that devotes a large share of its GDP to defense, more than 2%.
14. For a similar view see C. Iordanoglou and M. Matsaganis "Why Grexit cannot save Greece, But staying in the Euro area might" CES Open Forum Series 2017–2018 Center for European Studies Harvard 2018.

References

Amiel, D., & Hyppolite, P. A. (2016). Is there an Easy Way Out? Redenomination Issues and their Financial Consequences in Case of A Greek Exit from the Eurozone. In P. E. Petrakis (Ed.), *A New Growth Model for the Greek Economy*. Palgrave/Springer.

Bernstein, E. M. (1961). The New Administration and the Dollar Payments Problem. In S. E. Hariss (Ed.), *The Dollar in Crisis*. Harcourt Brace and World.

Blanchard, O., Erceg, C., & Linde, J. (2016). *Jump Starting the Euro Area Recovery: Would a Rise in Core Fiscal Spending Help the Periphery* (NBER, Macroeconomics Annual #31). MIT Press.

Christodoulakis, N. (2019). Greece and the Euro Area: The Cost of Weak Institutions, *Working Paper Series*, 19–08, November 2019, Athens University of Economics and Business

Dallara, C. H. (2024). *Euroshock*. Rodin Books.

Galbraith, J. K. (2016). *Welcome to the Poisoned Chalice*. Yale University Press.

Hardouvelis, G. (2015, July 7). Greece: How to Undo the Damage. *INY Times*.

IMF. (2012). *Greece: Request for Extended Arrangement Under the Extended Fund Facility: Staff Report* (Country Report 12/57). IMF.

IMF. (2014). *Greece: Fifth Review Under the Extended Fund Facility and Request for Waiver of Non-observance of Performance Criterion and Re-phasing of Access* (Staff Report 14/151). IMF.

IMF. (2016). *Germany: Report of the 2016 Article IV Consultation* (Country Report 16/202). IMF.

IMF. (2017). *Greece: Ex Post Evaluation of Exceptional Access Under the 2012 Extended Arrangement* (Country Report 17/44). IMF.

Iordanoglou, C., & Matsaganis, M. (2018). *Why Grexit Cannot Save Greece (But Staying in the Euro Area Might)*. CES Open Forum Series 2017–2018. Center for European Studies Harvard.

Kathimerini. (2015a, June 25). Marathon Discussions in Brussels.

Kathimerini. (2015b, July 7). Domestic Backing for PM's Last Gasp Effort.

Katsikas, D. (2024). Crises, Opportunities, and the Evolution of Greece's Growth Model in the EMU. *Social Sciences, 13*, 327. https://doi.org/10.3390/socsci13070327

Krugman, P. (2015, June 30). Greece over the Brink. *INY Times*.

Lazaretou, S. (2021). Greece in the EMU: Economic Benefits and Policy Constraints, Lessons Learned and Moving Forward. H*ellenic Review of European Law*, International Edition, 2021, 105–134.

Matsaganis, M. (2018). *The Contorted Politics of Guaranteed Minimum Income in Greece* (DAStU Working Papers – LPS-2/2018).

Matsaganis, M. with Leventi, C., & Flevotomou, M. (2024, November). *How Greece Became More Equal*. Bank of Greece.

Michalopoulos, C. (2012). *A Modern Greek Tragedy: The Final Act?* Letter to E. Herfkens.

Michalopoulos, C. (2017). *Aid, Trade and Economic Development: Fifty Years of Globalization*. Cham.

Michalopoulos, C. (2018). *Priorities for the Next Day*, (in Greek *Προταιρεοτητες για την Ερχομενη Μερα*, *Kathimerini*, August 5.

Michalopoulos, C. (2019, March 15). Little Hope Six Months After Bailouts. *Kathimerini*.

Orphanides, A. (2015). *The Euro Area Crisis Five Years After the Original Sin* (MIT Sloan Working Paper 5147-15). MIT.
Pagoulatos, G. (2020, April). EMU and the Greek Crisis: Testing the Extreme Limits of an Asymmetric Union. *Journal of European Integration*.
Papaconstantinou, G. (2015, July 9). Re Greece over the Brink. *INY Times*.
Papaconstantinou, G. (2016). *Game Over I Alithia ya tin crisi*. Papadopoulos.
PIIE. (2019). https://www.piie.com/microsites/greek-debt-crisis-no-easy-way-out. Accessed on 28 November 2024.
Schumacher, J., & Weder-di Mauro, B. (2015). *Greek Debt Sustainability and Official Crisis Lending*. Brookings Papers on Economic Activity 2015. Brookings.
Stiglitz, J. E. (2015, July 25). Greece, the Sacrificial Lamb. *INY Times*.
Tsoukalis, L. (2023). *Europe's Coming of Age*, Polity Press
Varoufakis, Y. (2017). *Adults in the Room*. Vintage.
World Bank. (2017). *World Development Indicators*. World Bank.
Wyplosz, C., & Sgherri, S. (2016). *The IMF's Role in Greece in the Context of the 2010 Standby* (IEO Background Paper BP-16/02-11). IMF.

CHAPTER 8

Greece and the EU: Present and Future

Introduction

In early 2020, I was visiting Greece again and felt that the time was ripe for Greece to get a 'New Deal' in its debt from its Eurozone partners (Michalopoulos, 2020). It did not happen then and it still has not. Little did I know at the time, January 30, 2020, that the world was about to enter several years of tremendous economic upheaval as a result, of the COVID-19 pandemic.

The pandemic depressed incomes and changed global economic relations, in ways that could not have anticipated at the time. It also resulted in changes in the Eurozone rules that strengthened its capacity to assist countries in distress. This chapter reviews developments in Greece and its relations with the Eurozone starting with the ascent of the Mitsotakis government in June 2019 to the present. It then looks ahead and outlines the main challenges facing the Greek economy and, how its membership in the Eurozone, can help address them.

Economic Performance 2019–2025

In reviewing the Greek economy in 2017, I had written that on the Greek side "the only option it has, if it wants to stay in the euro, is to demonstrate political stability and for the government, whichever government, to stay on course and to do what it has agreed to do for the three

C. Michalopoulos, *Greek Foreign Trade and Finance*, Palgrave Studies in Economic History, https://doi.org/10.1007/978-3-031-92104-9_8

years of the current program. Besides the rising debt burden, the only other constant of the last decade has been Greek political instability: five parliamentary elections in six years and eight ministers of finance do not promote confidence to investors either domestic or foreign" (Michalopoulos, 2017, p. 272).

When I returned to Greece in January 2020, the political stability that I had sought had materialized. I argued that, "as shown by the largely positive reports of all the surveillance missions the Greek governments have done their part" (Michalopoulos, 2020). The Tsipras government had done its part in maintaining fiscal austerity for four years (notwithstanding some slippage at the end of its tenure) as well as introducing a number of policy reforms aimed at reducing inequality. According to both the IMF and the last Commission report the Mitsotakis government has made a good start in most cases—good enough for the Commission to conclude in its last Enhanced Surveillance Report last November that 'Greece has taken the necessary actions to achieve its specific reform commitments for 2019' (Michalopoulos, 2020). The government had also launched a major study that outlined a growth strategy for the Greek economy with a large number of recommendations of how to achieve it (Pissarides et al., 2023).

I felt that much more should be done, especially to revitalize investment, as Greece was last in the EU in the share of GDP devoted to Gross Fixed Capital Formation (GFCF), and that a lot had to be done by the Greek government. I pointed out that only 37.5% of the funds budgeted from the European Structural Investment Fund six years before had been spent and 7 billion euro provided by the EU under the 2014–2020 program had yet to be contracted and may be lost. I concluded that, "The time has come for a new deal: The Europeans should be more relaxed about getting repaid and be willing to lessen the requirement of running a large primary budget surplus. In exchange, the Greek government should explicitly commit itself to a target of increasing the amounts it spends on investment" (Michalopoulos, 2020).

Then the pandemic descended everywhere and everything changed. The Greek government, as many other governments around the world, had to run large deficits in both 2020 and 2021, prior to restoring equilibrium in 2022 and achieving a primary surplus again in 2023. GDP declined in 2020 but stabilized in 2021 and started to grow again in 2022.

The government increased COVID-19-related spending by 18% of GDP—much higher than the EU average of 10%—though the results in terms of mortality were not that great: Greece's mortality from COVID-19 of 327 per 100,000 of population, placed it 9th highest in the EU, despite its favorable climate conditions—probably as a result of weaknesses in the health system.[1]

When the pandemic emergency hit the European Union, the Union responded relatively quickly in two different ways: First, "learning from the incoherent experience of austerity in response to the Great recession in the early 2010s allowed a change of course towards a remarkably assertive EU wide welfare COVID-19 response in 2020" (Hemerijck & Matsaganis, 2024, p. 10).

Second, and as part of this response, the EU established the Recovery and Resilience Facility (RRF) scheduled to provide 650 billion Euro (359 billion grants and 291 billion loans) to help countries through projects that would help get them out of the COVID-19-related crisis and make their societies more sustainable and resilient. For the first time ever, the RRF is funded by the European Commission borrowing on the capital markets on behalf of the EU as a whole. This was a major step forward in economic integration perhaps agreed to by the conservative North as this emergency had hit all EU countries and not only the ones with weak governments and institutions. In deference to the sensitivities of some of its members, the RRF is labeled a 'temporary instrument' (https://Commission.europa.eu). This time "without conscious intent, the governance of the Euro matured and greater fiscal and monetary discretion allowed, while the ECB promise to save the single currency clashed with rules based ordoliberal orthodoxy" (Hemerijk & Matsaganis, 2024, p. 275). Greece's original share of the RRF was to be 30.5 billion Euro by 2026—but it was subsequently increased (see below).

Global economic performance significantly exceeded expectations in 2023 and 2024, as everybody seemingly had anticipated a global recession that did not happen: Inflation was curbed while output and employment rose globally. In late 2023, the *Economist* published its annual review of the economic performance of OECD countries (*The Economist*, 2023). Subtitled 'Another unlikely triumph' and 'From the ruins' it showed that for the second year in a row, the Greek economy performed best in the OECD. This is a remarkable achievement given that, exactly a decade ago, the Greek economy was in the midst of a debt crisis, unemployment stood at 29%, and there was plenty of Grexit talk.

The five indicators the *Economist* used to assess performance included two pertaining to inflation, change in core prices and inflation breadth; growth in GDP and employment, and change in stock market share prices. Greece ranked number one in increase in share prices, did exceptionally well (top five) in containing inflation, pretty well in GDP growth (11th) and worse in employment growth (15th). The *Economist* noted that the Greek economy was 'until recently a byword for mismanagement' and that the IMF praised the government in its Article IV consultation for its efforts to promote the digital transformation of the economy and enhancing market competition (IMF, 2024).

In reviewing the performance of the Greek economy over the last decade, a few things stand out: Political stability has been reestablished and—much to my surprise and expectation—the old political party duo of New Democracy and PASOK has reemerged from the 2012 ashes, as SYRIZA has imploded. The Mitsotakis government has also introduced a number of reforms, some recommended by the Pissarides report (Pissarides et al., 2023) to strengthen the pension system and competition, improve the administration of social assistance, as well as increase digitalization. It has also had to manage a series of problems caused by the influx of illegal immigrants as well as deal with other territorial issues raised by an assertive Turkiye.

The debt/GDP ratio has been lowered to an estimated 153% at the end of 2024 (EU November 2024 forecast) below pandemic levels—thanks both to GDP growth and increased inflation. The banking system has been strengthened by divesting its large portfolio of non-performing loans, but an IMF report (IMF, 2022) notes that banks need to increase their resilience against future risks. By the end of 2024 Greek government bonds were raised to investment grade level by the four rating agencies, thus, in a way, both reflecting and confirming the euphoric performance of the stock market.

The economy maintained its strong growth in 2024 with real GDP rising by 2.3% among the highest in the EU. Despite the good recent performance, Greek GDP per capita is still below pre-crisis levels. Almost 19% of its population are below the poverty line, compared to 14% in the EU (World Bank, 2024a). Unemployment has come down from the staggering late 2013 levels of 28.9% to 9.5% in late 2024, a historic low since 2009 (IMF, 2025a p. 12) but still almost double the EU average.

The government ran again a fiscal surplus amounting to about 2.3% of GDP in 2024 and is expected to continue at that rate for the medium term. As a result of this performance, the IMF, in its most recent consultation, projected that the debt to GDP ratio will fall to below 130% by 2030 (IMF, 2025a p. 36). All this is obviously good news in some respects. At the same time, spending on social assistance is the lowest as a percent of GDP in the euro area (IMF, 2022, p. 13). Greece entered the debt crisis with higher income inequality than many EU members. Inequality indices improved during the crisis and the pandemic, but deteriorated again after 2021. The latest indicators showed that, while still higher, inequality at a Gini coefficient of around 0.33 is still slightly higher than the euro area median.

The IMF 2025 IMF staff mission supported the government's commitment to continue to run primary budget surpluses at around 2.3% of GDP and referred again to the need to address the 'structural' problems facing the Greek economy. These include the usual suspects—the sclerotic judicial system, tax evasion in the large informal sector and the self-employed and the still low level of both domestic savings and investment; as well as the new challenges arising from the low levels of labor participaton and the need to address climate change (IMF, 2025a).

The broad question before the Greek society is what must be done to address the long-term challenges facing Greece and how can its EU membership help in meeting them. In my view, the Greek economy faces fundamental problems that affect the long run supply and quality of both factors of production: labor and capital, as well as long-standing problems in foreign trade. In particular, there is a demographic time bomb which will dominate the labor market and which together with raising investment for equitable and sustainable growth are the two main challenges facing Greek society in the coming decade. These challenges have implications for Greek foreign trade and finance that in turn involve the relationship of Greece with the European Union. At the same time, the European Union itself is facing global challenges and this will raise questions about how Greece fits in with an evolving Union.

The Next Decade[2]

Labor

Europe's population is shrinking and aging. Greece is among the leaders in both: The fertility rate in the EU is below 2.0 and in Greece, at 1.4, among the lowest, despite a recent uptick. Greece's working age population declined by 0.7% per annum in the last decade and is projected to decline by 1% per annum until 2030 (IMF, 2024, p. 16). The dependency ratio for old age is currently at 39% compared to an EU average of 33% and is projected to go to 42% by 2027 and an almost impossible 75% by 2050 (OECD, 2024).

The problem with pensions is already here: Greece spends 16% of its GDP on pensions—the highest in the EU while the share of social assistance spending at 8% of GDP is among the lowest in the EU. In per capita terms, it was next to last, Latvia (IMF, 2022, p. 14). The result of this allocation of resources is that while the combination has helped reduce income inequality before taxes and transfers, it is an inefficient way of doing so, as pensions are not as well targeted as social assistance.

The implications of demographic change for the labor market are equally obvious: given the increase in the old-age group and the decline in labor force, the dependency ratio has to increase unless there is a very large increase in the labor force participation rate and/or there is net immigration—especially of young people.

The labor force participation rate, at 52% is among the lowest in the EU; that of women at 45% is lower (World Bank, 2024b). The most recent IMF report suggests a small increase in the female participation rate in 2024 but recommends increases in child care and elderly care facilities so that women can "engage more productively in the economy" (IMF, 2025b p. 2). While the existence of a large informal sector suggests a downward bias in the participation rate estimates, it is clear that additional social spending in childcare facilities is absolutely necessary, otherwise raising the employment rate may adversely affect the already low fertility rate.

Unfortunately, the migration story is also grim. While the international press and human rights organizations have rightly focused on the abominable conditions prevailing in Greece's detention centers for asylum seekers, and the government has rightly sought an improved EU-wide policy toward migrants, Greece has been suffering from net loss of migrants. Over the last decade, Greece net migration was negative—with tens of thousands of Greek workers—as well as undocumented foreigners moving out of Greece to the EU and beyond. Greece has the highest unemployment rate among high-educated workers (around 12%) in the eurozone, which also drove emigration during the crisis years 2010–2015. The statistics on such flows are not good, but there is considerable evidence of Greek professionals migrating to Western Europe—especially Germany. The issue has attracted attention as there are at least 3,000 Greek physicians operating in Germany, motivated by differences in employment conditions and health sector structure and policies (Golfinopoulos, 2017).

The Mitsotakis government has made a good start in passing a new law that improves security and stability for existing migrants and the new EU migration policy can also be expected to provide improved conditions for both new and existing migrants. Yet, a lot more needs to be done as will be discussed below.

Finally, small firms with low labor productivity dominate the economy. This is a very old story discussed in previous chapters. OECD estimates suggest labor productivity is about two-thirds of the OECD average. In the share of firms using high-speed internet, Greece ranks last (OECD, 2023, pp. 30, 43). Strengthening the labor market is necessary, both to raise labor productivity, and to keep highly trained professionals from migrating.

Capital

There are two aspects to the story about investment: private and public. On the private side, the absence of a developed capital market combined with occasional bouts of inflation, had made Greeks channel their private savings to housing. The typical Greek family of modest means would own a house in the traditional village or the islands and an apartment in Athens or another urban area—much to the chagrin of ordinary German taxpayers who thought they were being unfairly asked to bailout rich spendthrift Greek capitalists during the debt crisis. Over time, the situation improved with the development of capital markets and improved monetary stability. Still, the latest available estimates showed that the household savings rate of 7.1% is the lowest in the EU and obviously needs to be addressed urgently (IMF, 2022, p. 65).

The problems of doing business are well known. The last World Bank survey done in 2019 placed Greece last among the OECD and 79th place globally (World Bank, 2021). The government has done a few things to reduce red tape and various Greek governments have tried to boost levels by providing incentives to foreign investors that have resulted in significant inflows e.g. the port of Pireaus, and many new ones under construction, e.g. the development of the old airport near Athens. The existing 'golden visa' regime has been recently modified, doubling to 800,000 euros the amounts that need to be invested to purchase housing in selected areas. However, the scheme creates few jobs and, despite the legal limitations, the properties are often used for short-term rentals—aggravating housing shortages for young people. As in the past, the role of public sector investment has been and will be critical.

The story about government investment was disappointing, is currently improving, but still has a long way to go in order to meet Greece's future challenges. As noted earlier, all recent economic assessments have stressed the importance of raising public sector investment. The latest estimates show that the public sector GFC is only 5% of GDP much lower than the EU average. The Mitsotakis government had not improved significantly the utilization of EU funds in recent periods—with these funds averaging only about 10% of GFC (see Table 6.3). Most recent reports suggest improvements in this area as well. However, much more needs to be done.

There are tremendous needs to address the challenges of climate change. First, Greece has a very large coastal area—the third largest in Europe, requiring investment in littoral communities to deal with rising water levels. Second, the country is prone to wildfires, which require investments to prevent future catastrophes as well as dealing with inevitable disasters, and third, there are large needs for investments in green energy.

Yet, the most recent government projections discussed with the IMF show an actual decrease in public sector investment after 2026 (IMF, 2025a p. 32). This could be because that is when the EU investment funds end. However, the needs for public investment, will, if anything, rise to establish a green economy. This will involve both increases in public sector investment and raising the carbon price that the government is committed to do. Raising the carbon price will adversely affect the poor as they spend more of their income on energy-intensive goods—which will give rise to additional needs for social transfers. For long-term sustainable growth, it is necessary to continue efforts to improve tax collection, reduce to the barest minimum the government budget primary surplus and increase rather than decrease flows to public sector investment and spending on social services.

Foreign Trade and Finance

The challenges of the next decade will be similar to the ones facing the Greek economy today, except for additional complications resulting from the introduction of the EU-wide carbon tax and the unpredictability of a more protectionist US under Trump. The current account is likely to continue to be in deficit and the challenge will be to fill it with private direct investment as well as maintain a good credit rating and access to the EU capital markets. The policies that would achieve this are the same as those needed to maintain a fiscal balance which is neither too restrictive nor damaging to Greece's creditworthiness and to improve the environment for private sector investment whether domestic or foreign.

Foreign trade policy is determined at the EU level. Hence, there are serious limits to what individual countries can do to promote exports. As Greece has a very small share of exports relative to its GDP, there is a temptation to suggest that export promotion agencies can correct this problem (Pissarides et al., 2023, p. 258). They obviously can be of some help but they are not likely to be determinant of overall performance, and in a country like Greece, where there is a tendency of cronyism, there are obvious dangers of trying to pick winners by supporting friends. The best way to promote exports is through general policies that increase productivity and reduce bureaucratic hassles. Thus, no specific recommendations about how to improve the balance of merchandise trade are made in the action program below.

An Action Program

Addressing the needs for a green and inclusive growth of an aging society while maintaining fiscal sustainability requires a set of mutually reinforcing reforms in many areas. The Pissarides Report (Pissarides et al., 2023) made a very large number of useful recommendations to improve a wide range of institutions and policies, including the system of education, public administration, the judicial system, social protection, as well as fiscal and foreign trade policy. While one may not agree with all of these recommendations, they are a useful basis for moving forward and the Greek government has already started to implement some of them. Migration policy is the one area that the report has not explicitly addressed, but which will be affected by policies affecting education and the labor market. In what follows I focus on action in four priority areas: (a) the labor market; (b) social services; (c) migration; (d) investment.[3]

The Labor Market

The Mitsotakis government has taken some important steps to streamline the pension system, reduce some benefits and raise the retirement age through a major reform enacted in 2020. EU projections suggest that under certain assumptions about employment, labor force participation, GDP and productivity growth, these reforms could reduce the Pension/GDP ratio by several percentage points by 2070 (EU, 2021). In the years until 2030, the net improvement in the pension/GDP ratio would be small, as the increased dependency ratio, would be just offset by reduced benefits and stricter rules on early pensions. In the later years, an important dimension of the reform is that the mandatory retirement age for both men and women would be adjusted for projected changes in life expectancy.[4] The problem however is that the projections depend critically on an increase in the labor participation rate for both men and women. For example, the total participation rate is supposed to increase by four percentage points in the decade 2020–2030. Nothing in the pension reform as such would help accomplish this.

In connection with increasing the participation of women in the labor force as well as close an existing gender gap in wages, a stricter implementation of laws against gender discrimination may be needed (Pissarides, 2023, p. 8). Increasing spending on children will both serve a social need and will help increase labor force participation of women. The development of a system of preschool care and education, with universal access from the age of six months can contribute to achieving both objectives.

Both labor productivity and mobility between jobs will also need to increase as a consequence of changes needed to promote the 'green' economy transition. This will require active labor market policies involving additional spending on training both for employed and unemployed especially in the sectors involved in the transition.

Social Assistance and Social Services

As noted earlier, an important government objective should be to increase the share of the GDP and the budget that goes to social assistance and social services, as they tend to support decreases both in poverty and in income inequality. In particular, it is important to:

- Expand healthcare coverage, strengthen the public sector health facilities and economize on the costs of medicines and supplies: Because public sector facilities are inadequate, in Greece private expenditures account for 40% of expenditures on health, the fourth highest proportion in the EU. There is a need to improve the quality of hospital care, as well as rationalize the system of procurement of pharmaceuticals and medical supplies giving greater priority to the provision of generics (Pissarides, 2023, p. 8)
- Provide support to low-income families that would be adversely affected by the introduction of a carbon tax.
- Increase spending and improve the system for caring for the elderly.
- Improve the structure and targeting of social benefits so that they do not provide disincentives for employment.

Migration

In the context of the new EU policy on migrants and refugees, the government needs to develop a national plan that has three dimensions:

- the quantity and skills of new immigrants that need to be added to the labor force;
- the investment and recurrent costs of integrating refugees and/or illegal immigrants into the economy;
- simplification of requirements for providing permanent residence and citizenship status for new immigrants.

A useful proposal aimed at planning and regulating the flow of new immigrants and refugees into the EU by using local governments of cities and municipalities to identify needs for additional labor has been put together (Schwan, 2023). However, applying this to Greece will need to take account of specific characteristics of the Greek economy: labor demand in agriculture and tourism, the two main sectors where much more labor is likely to be needed, is highly seasonal and local authorities have limited capacity to do serious planning.

Investment

The demands for climate adaptation and helping create a green economy require large amounts of public sector investment (see below). The tourism sector Greece's 'heavy industry' also requires additional investment in infrastructure in order to continue to expand. Any reasonable growth scenario for the next decade would require a substantial increase in public sector investment.

Private sector investment needs to increase as well. The most important step in this area is to reduce the regulatory and administrative burdens, which result from the complexity and the lack of transparency of the institutional framework for doing business.

The Future European Union

Greece's agenda for action depends significantly on steps taken by the Greek government and Greek society. However, such action is not going to take place in a vacuum: Greece will continue to be part of the EU and will need to implement EU-wide policies which themselves will evolve over time. Some of these policies have already been agreed and will be implemented in the future; others have yet be agreed but may be the subject of future deliberations in the EU as the EU itself adapts to developments in the global economy or are part of the evolving agenda for deeper integration.

In the aftermath of the pandemic, EU economies recovered slowly and Germany was still in recession through 2024. The Ukraine war created additional challenges by necessitating changes in the sources of energy supply that resulted in increased costs to European industry. More recently, the results of the US election created additional uncertainties about global policies in defense, trade and climate.

The EU recently commissioned two major studies on EU policies to meet future challenges: First, the Spanish and Belgian Presidencies commissioned Enrico Letta's *Much More than a Market* (Letta, 2024) that focused on reforms of the single market necessary to meet the future challenges of an equitable and sustainable growth. Second, the EU

Commission sponsored Mario Draghi's *The Future of European Competitiveness* (Draghi, 2024). The European Council of November 8, 2024 invited the Commission to present a new and comprehensive strategy on the deepening of the single market, including a roadmap with clear timelines and milestones (EU Council, 2024). Both studies contain important recommendations on a number of issues of relevance to the future of the Greek economy.

The Letta study, published in April 2024, focuses on reforms of the single market to extend its coverage to three sectors, finance, electronic communications and energy. These sectors had been kept outside the integration process, because they were considered too strategic for their operation and regulation to extend beyond national borders. Even within the original perimeter, the single market is in need of an overhaul: particularly, the intra-EU provision of services continues to encounter significant barriers that need to be addressed and removed to unlock the full potential of the single market (Letta, 2024, p. 4).

The Draghi report published in September, 2024 concludes that the EU is losing international competitiveness in global markets because of lower labor productivity growth, and that the relatively small size of European firms (because of different national regulations) does not permit them to enjoy economies of scale—thereby handicapping them in global competition with US and Chinese producers. Among the Report's many recommendations are proposals to raise productivity through more training as well as improved technology through increased expenditures on research and development, and that all these proposals would require significant increases in both public and private investment. In many respects, the report sounds as if it was talking specifically about problems facing Greek industry and more generally the Greek economy.

It is unclear how many of the recommendations in the two reports will actually be implemented. The Draghi report proposal to finance EU-wide projects through a permanent Eurobond facility produced the predictable outcry from the usual suspects in Germany, the Netherlands and elsewhere. However, it is clear that Europe is facing important challenges and that consideration will be given to strengthening co-operation in funding activities across the EU.

Climate

The EU has the world's largest carbon-pricing system, the emissions trading system (ETS). Emissions pricing is designed to encourage reductions in carbon emissions in the atmosphere by industries. While these policies help address the long-term global challenge of reducing emissions, they put EU industries at a disadvantage vis-a-vis their foreign competitors and/or may stimulate their move to other countries which do not tax carbon emissions. As a result, the EU has decided to establish a new carbon border adjustment mechanism (CBAM) which will require EU importers, as of January 1, 2026, to purchase certificates equivalent to the weekly EU carbon price. The CBAM will apply initially to imports in five emissions-intensive sectors deemed at greater risk of carbon leakage: cement, iron and steel, aluminum, fertilizers and electricity. The CBAM charge covers imports of these goods from all third countries other than those included in the ETS or a linked mechanism (European Parliament, 2023). Greece will have to introduce the appropriate administrative procedures to implement the new program.[5]

In addition, it is clear that climate change poses significant dangers for the management of the Greek economy. The most recent ESM annual report lists Greece as the country with the greatest exposure to hazards and the least coping capacity in all EU (ESM, 2024, p. 7). There are two issues in this area: first, the very large amounts of direct investment needed by both the public and the private sector to meet EU's climate targets by 2030. Annual investment needs are estimated at 350–650 billion euro or 2.6%–4.6% of EU GDP. While some of this could be funded by the private sector and part is expected to be financed under the Green Deal until 2027, substantial gaps remain (ESM, 2024, p. 18). Could the money raised through CBAM be earmarked for use in climate related investments or emergencies? (Tsoukalis, 2023, p. 121).

Second, there may be country needs for emergency finance to deal with catastrophic events like floods. It would seem appropriate for the EU to start considering the establishment of an emergency Fund that deals explicitly with climate related catastrophes.

Banking and Finance

The 2013 decision to establish an EU banking union was an important step in economic integration, as it established a common rule-book for all financial actors in the participating countries (Tsoukalis, 2023, p. 92). Subsequently, the EU created a new vehicle for addressing possible bank failures through the establishment of the Single Resolution Fund (SRF) in 2016. The Fund has 80 billion euro and has been helpful in addressing bank failures throughout the EU. There are two pending issues for strengthening the EU's capacity to deal with bank system failures. First, is the establishment of European Deposit Insurance Scheme. Practically everybody who has looked at the question of how to promote an integrated banking system has recommended such a scheme but it has not happened.

Second, there is a need to establish a backstop to the SRF. "This backstop, as shaped in the amended ESM Treaty, could provide up €68 billion in additional firepower in the event of the Single Resolution Fund's depletion. To implement the backstop, all euro-area member states must ratify the amended ESM Treaty, endorsed politically in early 2021. The lack of a backstop is a problem if the SRF is exhausted during a significant banking crisis" (ESM Managing Director, Annual Report, 2023).[6]

The Draghi report concludes that the EU relies too much on bank lending for private sector investment. In particular, it argues that it is difficult for inventors to find investors. "To unlock private capital, the EU must build a genuine Capital Markets Union (CMU). As a key pillar of the CMY, the European Securities and Market Authority should transition from a body that co-ordinates national regulators into a single common regulator for all European securities markets" (Draghi, 2024, p. 61). The Letta report calls for a significant transformation: the creation of a Savings and Investments Union developed from the incomplete Capital Markets Union (Letta, 2024, p. 11).

Investment

The current EU program under the Recovery and Resilience Facility is funded through 2026. It obviously needs to be continued. Although the problems created by the pandemic may have been addressed, the needs for climate change will still exist, as will the demands for helping poor regions. The Draghi report concludes that in order to meet EU objectives in improving labor productivity in the context of a green and equitable growth, an additional annual investment of 750–800 billion euro are needed which would be equivalent to raising the ratio of EU GFC to GDP from 22 to 27% (Draghi, 2024, p. 59). It is beyond the scope of this analysis to comment on the accuracy or feasibility of such a large increase. It is sufficient to recall in this context that in Greece, the GFC/GDP ratio is currently at 15%. Raising 5% points would be a gigantean task, but it has happened before, during the growth years half a century ago. Clearly, as noted earlier the ratio of investment to GDP must grow and some of it must continue to come from EU-wide programs.

Greece moved quickly to establish the National Recovery and Resilience Fund amounting to 30.5 billion euro (17.8 billion grants and 12.7 billion loans). On July 21, 2021, the program was approved by the EU Council and has been in operation since then. Its projects focus on four areas: (a) green transition; (b) digital transformation; (c) innovation-research and development; and (d) extroversion-presumably export orientation. Subsequently, the European Council increased the funding of the program to a total of 36 billion euro (18.2 grants, 17.7 loans) and approved a series of program changes requested by Greece (EU Council, 2025). There were some concerns, that the "program changed focus involving €1.35 billion out of the €36 billion of the Fund have been redirected to actions and projects that are undeniably important for society, but not so much for their contribution to improving the country's production model" (*Kathimerini*, 2025). One of the main themes emerging from all reviews of these programs has been the importance of expediting Greek government procedures in order to improve project implementation.

The Monetary Union

Several proposals have been made to strengthen the banking system through the SRF backstop and to establish a European deposit insurance system. There are also proposals to improve the functioning of the capital market, all of which can contribute to monetary stability. There have not been any proposals to improve the EMU as such. Only general suggestions have been made to apply the rules regarding fiscal discipline more flexibly—as they were during the pandemic, and a consensus has emerged that previous applications resulted in too much fiscal austerity.

There have always been calls for the establishment of a true fiscal union. However, I do not believe this is possible as long as there are national constitutional requirements linking national debt to GDP, as exist in Germany. There is always the problem of asymmetric adjustment between countries in consistent balance of payments surplus and those in deficit:

there is simply no way to establish rules in this matter outside of creating a full monetary and fiscal union. There is little chance that this will happen in the next decade, the time-frame of this analysis. But the uncertainty created by currrent geopolitical tensions calls for increased caution about all future predictions; and the EU has a record of responding well to crises...

Other Issues

Russia's aggressive behavior and questions about the new US government's commitment to European defense, raise a multitude of issues about new EU based integration initiatives in many areas of national security, access to supplies and the like, which are outside the scope of this analysis. There are a few such initiatives however of potential importance to Greece that may deserve additional consideration.

"European institutions have always felt uncomfortable with distributional issues. They wanted to believe that European integration was a win-win game for all, while social contracts remained mostly a matter for national governments" (Tsoukalis, 2023, p. 115). To some extent the COVID-19 response which involved a health sector intervention made a break from the political concerns of individual governments. Letta's report highlights the need to strengthen co-operation in health, especially in research, innovation and exchange of information (Letta, 2024, p. 7). Another issue that may be worth pursuing in the future would be a European unemployment re-insurance scheme. The purpose for such as a scheme would be to provide funding to countries that have experienced an external shock of some kind that has resulted in significant increase in unemployment (Tsoukalis, 2023, p. 125). Given the climate risks it faces, the Greek government may well be advised to seek to propose such a scheme.

Some Preliminary Conclusions

The last decade witnessed improvements both in Greek economic policy and in the operation of the EMU. Political stability in Greece combined with adherence to a strict—probably overly so, fiscal policy resulted in overcoming both the debt crisis and the pandemic. These actions helped restore access to the European capital markets, and modest growth in incomes, which however, have not returned to the pre-crisis levels. The

EMU has been strengthened and become more flexible thus making it more resilient and capable of supporting unforeseen disasters.

All this is especially welcome, as the international political and economic environment has drastically deteriorated. Wars in Europe's doorstep and in the Middle-East have poisoned the atmosphere for co-operation on global issues such as the climate crisis and poverty in poor countries. The role of the WTO in trade has diminished and the role of global institutions, such as the IMF and the World Bank, has been questioned. In this setting, Greece a small country in a geographically critical area with a European past, must cement its links and commitment to a future within the European Union—especially as the Union itself is being strengthened in order to help its members meet challenges of a sustainable and equitable future. This will require continued Greek dependence on the Union in ways and forms that need to evolve, as the Union itself is evolving. These issues and the lessons of the Greek history of economic dependence for other countries that may be considering links or association in larger groupings or entities are the subject of the concluding chapter.

Notes

1. Incidence of coronavirus (COVID-19) deaths in Europe as of January 13, 2023, by country *(per 100,000 population)* (https://www.statista.com) accessed 8 April 2024.
2. The main elements of the analysis in this section were presented in Michalopoulos (2024).
3. The main elements of the action program proposals were presented in Michalopoulos (2024).
4. It appears that legislation to this effect has been passed by the Greek parliament. However, the current and previous governments have not implemented it so far. Pension reform is very unpopular as recent experience in France has shown. But it will have to happen in Greece as well in the near future.
5. The Greek government has appointed the Directorate for Economic and Financial Crime in the Ministry of Economy and Finance as the 'contact' point for CBAM-one wonders why this is the appropriate unit.
6. Italy is the only country that has not ratified the agreement.

References

Draghi, M. (2024). *The Future of European Competitiveness*. European Commission. EU.

The Economist. (2023). Which Economy Did Best in 2023? https://www.economist.com/finance-and-economics/2023/12/17/which-economy-did-best-in-2023

ESM. (2023). *Annual Report 2023*. ESM.

EU. (2021). *The 2021 Aging Report: Economic and Budgetary Projections for the EU Member States (2019-2070)*. Greece. economy-finance.ec.europa.eu1b6d32b6-74bc-4343-9d16-f4386f5141afen

European Council. (2024, November 8). *Budapest Declaration on the New European Competitiveness Deal*. www.consilium.europa.eu

European Council. (2025, January 14). *Council Implementing Decision on Recovery and Resilience Plan for Greece*. www.consilium.europa.eu

European Parliament. (2023, June). *CBAM—Implications for Climate and Competition*. EPRS | European Parliamentary Research Service Author: Henrique Morgado Simões Members' Research Service PE 698.889.

Golfinopoulos, A. (2017). *The Migration of Greek Physicians to Germany: Motivations, Factors and the Role of National Health Sectors*. https://doi.org/10.18278/epa.2.2.8

Hemerijk, J. & M. Matsaganis, (2024). *Who's Afraid of the Welfare State Now?* Oxford University Press

IMF. (2022). *Greece: Selected Issues* (Country Report No.22/174). https://doi.org/10.5089/9798400213038.002

IMF. (2024). *Greece: Article IV Consultation* (Country Report No.24/23, Staff Report, p. 7). https://doi.org/10.5089/9798400263262.002

IMF. (2025a). *Greece: Article IV* (Country Report, 25/85).

IMF. (2025b). *Greece: Staff Concluding Statement of the 2025 Article IV Consultation Mission*. https://www.imf.org/en/News/Articles/2025/01/30/CS-Greece-2025

Kathimerini. (2025, January 28). Recovery and Resilience Fund Cash Going off Target.

Letta, E. (2024). *Much More Than a Market*. EU Commission.

Michalopoulos, C. (2017). *Aid Trade and Development*, Palgrave

Michalopoulos, C. (2020). *It's Time for a New Deal*. ekathimerini, January 20.

Michalopoulos, C. (2024). *The Greek Economy a Decade Later* (ELAMEP Policy Brief #189/2024).

OECD. (2023). *Greece:; Economic Policy Reform: Going for Growth* (pp. 30, 43). https://www.oecd.org/economy/greece-economic-snapshot/#:2023

OECD. (2024). *Old Age Dependency Ratio*. https://doi.org/10.1787/e0255c98-en. Accessed on 08 April 2024.

Pissarides, C., et al. (2023). *A Growth Strategy for the Greek Economy*. CEPR.

Raush, R. (2024). *Climate Change and Financial Stability*. ESM.
Schwan, G. (2023). *Towards a Humane Refugee Policy for the European Union*. https://feps-europe.eu/publication/towards-a-humane-refugee-policy-for-the-european-union
Tsoukalis, L. (2023). *Europe's Coming of Age*. Polity Press.
World Bank. (2021). *Ease of Doing Business Rank*. https://databank.worldbank.org/source/doing-
World Bank. (2024a). https://pip.worldbank.org/country-profiles/GRC. Accessed on 10 April 2024.
World Bank. (2024b). *Gender Data Portal*. https://genderdata.worldbank.org/countries/greece

CHAPTER 9

The Future of Economic Dependence

Introduction

Almost exactly two centuries ago, a small group of Greek rebels asked citizens in Western Europe for financial support of their struggle for independence from the Ottoman Empire. Some responded by buying bonds of the emerging nation because of its connection to ancient Greece, the cradle of democracy. And so started an economic dependence that has lasted to this day.

The Greek nation benefited greatly from its links with the Great Powers of Europe, including Russia. In pursuit of their own interests, these Powers, helped Greece'a economy and supported the expansion of its territory. The road was bumpy, as the Great Powers had often fallen out among themselves posing difficult choices for Greece. In the post-World War II era, Greece has committed itself to European integration which has many dimensions, of which the economic links related to trade and finance form only one component.

As this is being written, democracy is in retreat in many parts of the globe. It is gone almost completely in Russia—where it had never really caught on. Geopolitical conflict undermines international collaboration; wars are raging in many places including again involving Crimea, and a new US administration seems committed to policies that appear likely to undermine old alliances and create more economic uncertainty. On top of this, long-term changes in technology and climate are forcing change

C. Michalopoulos, *Greek Foreign Trade and Finance*, Palgrave Studies in Economic History, https://doi.org/10.1007/978-3-031-92104-9_9

whether societies like it or not. In this very challenging and almost chaotic environment, Greece must consider the reforms needed to address many structural economic weaknesses as well as the policies involving its links to and economic dependence on the European Union that will promote equitable and sustainable economic growth. Economic dependence is only one of many aspects of foreign policy, especially political links and defense issues which are outside the scope of this study. This volume has focused on two aspects of this multifaceted dependence, trade and finance which will be considered below.

Trade

After several decades of participation in the Common Market, it is fair to say that Greece has not exploited fully the opportunities offered by duty-free entry of its products in the very large European market. The EU market which has lost the UK but has added a lot of other countries, absorbs about 50% of Greek exports, about the same three decades ago. There is strong evidence that the competitiveness of Greek firms has eroded partly as a result of the prevalence of small enterprises with very slow growth in productivity. Efforts to increase exports should continue to focus on 'horizontal' policies that promote competitiveness and reduce the administrative burden to exporters much as recommended in the Pissarides report (Pisarides, 2023, p. 258). Vertical policies supporting particular sectors should be limited to new start-ups with high value added products and new technology potential.

New EU-wide initiatives to liberalize trade in services should be welcomed. But emphasis should be placed on strengthening the tourism sector, both through infrastructure investments and through programs that encourage year-round arrivals.

Perhaps the most important benefit that Greece would enjoy in trade through its EU membership is the defensive one: The EU by virtue of the total size of its market and its common policy is a major actor in global trade policy making. The EU can give cover to and counter new protection efforts initiated by the new US administration. The greatest danger to global trade is the competitive introduction of increased tariff protection in major markets such as the US, the EU and China, which will result in substantial increases in global poverty.

Investment

Greece's EU membership should be helpful in raising the level of public sector investment needed for long-term sustainable growth. The current EU program ends in 2026, but there is a good chance that it will continue based on the recommendations of the Draghi report, and Greece can be expected to be a beneficiary. Hopefully, such a program will be funded by Euro-wide bonds. The focus of the public sector investments should be as proposed above on the social sectors, improving labor productivity, climate and tourist infrastructure. The idea of using the EU's Carbon Border Adjustment Mechanism (CBAM) revenues to fund climate abatement is worth exploring in this connection. But attention needs also to be directed to measures that increase foreign direct investment.

The traditional calculations presented earlier in this volume showed that Greece has been a net beneficiary of transfers from the EU. This was because the transfers of funds for various investment programs plus what was provided to agriculture exceeded the contributions Greece was making to the EU budget. These calculations may need to be reformulated as Greece is paying back large official loans it received from EU institutions *with interest.*

I have argued frequently that saddling Greece with large debts to EU governments and institutions, originally to save commercial banks in France and Germany, was a drag on future Greek growth as it has necessitated fiscal austerity for decades. The amount of debt outstanding to the EU countries and official institutions at the end of 2024 is around 230 billion euro, more than 60% of its total debt burden. 190.8 billion euro is due to the ESM of which the bulk is an EFSF loan of 129 billion whose repayment stretches to 2070. Then there is about 40 billion left of the original Greek Loan Facility debt to 14 EU countries whose maturity has been extended to 2041.

The total Greek debt/GDP ratio is projected to decline further in the years ahead, making its debt sustainable according to IMF projections. The debt to the European institutions has long maturities and low interest rates. However, total interest payments are going to increase from about 7 billion euro in 2024 to 9 billion in 2028 (IMF, 2024, Table 3) crowding out investment which at the same time is projected to decline. This makes no sense in terms of Greece's priorities.

Greece will have to pay 40 billion in interest to EU governments and institutions over the next several decades of which 30 billion to ESM and the remainder 10 billion to EU governments.

First, it would seem appropriate to subtract these amounts of interest paid from future calculation of 'net transfers' by the EU to Greece. The policy question is whether Greece should seek further debt relief on these loans. My personal opinion is that it should do so at some point with regard to the 10 billion euro that it is supposed to pay in interest to EU governments under the Greek Loan Facility, but not on the loans from the ESFS and the MSA, as these would appear to undermine the financial viability of the EU institutions.

Reforms aimed at increasing integration of EU capital markets as well as reducing and streamlining conflicting national regulatory regimes in order to promote private sector investment, should also be of great help to the Greek economy. Questions will arise about the implications of these reforms for the Athens Stock Exchange, but the key issue should be whether and how to promote private green-field investment and inventor-investor connection.

Continued access to the European capital markets will be central to managing the economy and the balance of payments. The policies that will ensure such access involve fundamental questions about fiscal and monetary policy under the EMU and are discussed in more detail below.

The EMU

Membership in the EU will yield obvious benefits as the EU moves closer to becoming a true banking union. Establishment of a deposit insurance scheme will be of great help in a country that has had a number of banks with shaky balance sheets.

Earlier discussion in this volume raised a variety of issues about the functioning of the EMU and the need to deal with inherent asymmetries in its structure. The experience of the past decade, including the pandemic, suggests several, in retrospect obvious, conclusions. Both fiscal and monetary policy are critical in addressing domestic and external imbalances. Monetary policy encounters serious difficulties when there are significant fiscal policy divergencies among members. And the monetary union encounters fundamental asymmetries when there is no fiscal union and there are is no way to rectify imbalances by pressuring adjustment both of countries with external surpluses and deficits. There is no way to ensure that surplus countries like Germany are going to run a deficit to accommodate adjustment in Greece or other countries in the EU periphery. Germany's lackluster economic performance in the last several years has increased calls for a change in its constitutional provision that limits its budget deficits to 0.35% of GDP. It appears that recent action by the German parliament will introduce some flexibility to this rule. Whether this can be used as a basis for moving toward greater integration of Europe-wide fiscal policy is unclear at this point. What Greece can do however, is to improve its regulations and climate for investment so as to induce more foreign direct investment from Germany or other surplus countries.

Given, (a) that there is little likelihood of the EMU moving toward a fiscal union or, for that matter, pressuring traditionally surplus countries to adjust; and (b) that Greece is likely to continue to have a current account deficit in the foreseeable future, there is at least a need for a simplification of the fiscal rules to make them more flexible, realistic and operative. The new rules should be credible, so as to strengthen market confidence. They should not require complex and time consuming treaty amendment processes (Lazaretou, 2021, p. 19). The new fiscal policy rules adopted by the EU last year are a step in the right direction (EU Council 2024). The main novelty in these rules has to do with setting adjustment toward equilibrium which will not be uniform for every country but will be adapted to the characteristics of each country through negotiations between the Commission and each member state, which must be endorsed by the EU Council (CSIS, 2024).

It remains to be seen how these rules will be applied in practice. Obviously, in the case of Greece (and some others, like Italy) such policies must include concerns about debt sustainability. But does that mean that the Greek government has to run a primary surplus forever? If not, what is the delicate balance that maintains access to the private capital markets at a reasonable cost, as well as provides for public sector investment needed for sustainable and equitable growth as well as caring for an aging population? These are the difficult questions that Greek governments have to answer in the next decade.

Implications for Others

The Greek experience has important implications for other small countries in Europe's periphery considering membership or emerging economies elsewhere in the world which are considering various forms of economic integration. There are two different levels of integration for which the experience is relevant: (a) participation in a customs union, with freedom of movement for goods and services, as well as labor; (b) participation in a monetary union.

The challenges of a customs union are substantial but relatively straightforward and many emerging economies are participating in such arrangements with various levels of economic integration. The most important lesson from the Greek experience is that small open economies in Europe's periphery should strengthen their institutions before joining. The same is true for other emerging economies considering integration efforts in Sub-Sahara Africa or elsewhere. In connection with joining custom union, it is very important to remove bureaucratic or other obstacles to trade. Establishing a trade promotion institution can also be helpful, provided it is possible to establish guard-rails that prevent cronyism and nepotism.

The institutional demands for joining a monetary union and, in particular the EU, are much greater. Joining a fixed rate regime or a monetary union led by strong economies requires very prudent fiscal policies as well as a recognition that the monetary policy pursued by the monetary union at any point in time may not be appropriate for each individual member. Further, that there are asymmetries in the adjustment process to external disequilibria, with the burden of adjustment falling primarily on countries in deficit. Careful consideration of the implications of existing fiscal policy rules and the flexibilities they provide is critical to a decision for participating in this or any other monetary union. The Greek experience offers a valuable lesson for peripheral countries considering entry into a monetary union. While the potential benefits of easy and cheap borrowing are evident, there are significant challenges in fiscal management and policy adjustment in a constantly changing global environment.

Another set of issues has to do with the availability of financing. In this connection, there are two kinds of financing that should be available: First, there should be financing for long-term development purposes, from a regional development bank such as the EIB or similar entity available to the members of the integrating group of countries. In addition, there should be financing on reasonable terms available for short-term balance of payments disturbances resulting from unforeseen calamities or emergencies.

The Only Option

In the past two hundred years, Europe's Great Powers, each pursuing its own national interest, provided political, military and economic support to Greece. The ensuing relations were not always smooth. Greece's dependence on Europe led to the creation of domestic political parties, factions or movements, each identified with the interests of an individual or group of European powers. This created political problems in Greece when the interests of the European powers diverged as they did on several occasions: during the Crimean war, when England and France supported the Ottoman Empire against Russia; during World War I when the Greek King's links to Germany led for a time to Greek neutrality and resulted in a military intervention by the Entente powers; and in the aftermath of World War II when the split between the pro-Russian Greek communist party and the rest of Greece's political parties who aligned with the US and its European allies led to the Greek civil war.

On the economic front, in the nineteenth and early twentieth centuries problems arose from Greece's continued armed conflicts with the Ottoman Empire as well as mismanagement of its fiscal affairs resulting in defaults on loans which had been floated in European markets, primarily the UK and France. Ultimately the European powers forced Greece to accept an international commission which controlled its finances for a decade ensuring repayment of the outstanding loans but also causing damage to Greece's economy and foreign trade.

In the aftermath of World War II, as Europe's economies lay in ruins, Greece's economic dependence moved for a short time to the US. The latter provided substantial amounts of economic assistance until Greece acted to secure a place in the European Community which has been a source of economic support for more than sixty years, except for a short interlude during the reign of the Greek junta.

Relations with the European powers became problematic when Greece joined the EMU. In developments eerily reminiscent of the situation in the late nineteenth century, Greece's lax fiscal policy and easy credit available from European and Greek banks combined with inadequate guard-rails and asymmetries in the functioning of the EMU led to a debt crisis. The initial EU reaction was punitive and intent primarily on protecting the interests of the European powers own banking system rather than focusing on remedies for Greece. Subsequent bail outs and strengthening of the EU financial support system combined with an unnecessarily harsh fiscal adjustment forced on Greece, resulted in restoring equilibrium and ultimately modest growth.

The EU took important steps to design a constructive region-wide response to the COVID-19 crisis. As noted in earlier chapters, these steps and others currently being considered hold promise for the future evolution of the capacity of European institutions to help address long-term economic challenges or problems resulting from emergencies. "For the overwhelming majority among Greek politicians and the Greek public at large, Europe, unpleasant and punishing though it can be—and Greeks are always good at finding excuses to grumble and blame others for their misfortunes- is the only option available" (Tsoukalis, 2023, p. 13).

Greek governments need to ensure that they learn from the lessons of the past and work with their European counterparts to strengthen European integration and institutions based on the many suggestions contained in European and Greek studies referred to in this volume. It is only through a European oriented future that Greece can meet the long-term challenges of an equitable and sustainable growth for its people.

References

CSIS. (2024). https://www.csis.org/analysis/new-european-fiscal-rules

EU Council. (2024). https://www.consilium.europa.eu/en/press/press-releases/2024/04/29/economic-governance-review-council-adopts-reform-of-fiscal-rules/

Lazaretou, S. (2021). Greece in the EMU: Economic Benefits and Policy Constraints, Lessons Learned and Moving Forward. In *Hellenic Review of European Law* (pp. 105–134). International Edition.

Pisarides, C., et al. (2023). A Growth Strategy for the Greek Economy CEPR

Tsoukalis, L. (2023). *Europe's Coming of Age*. Polity Press.

Index

C. Michalopoulos, *Greek Foreign Trade and Finance*, Palgrave Studies in Economic History, https://doi.org/10.1007/978-3-031-92104-9

The manufacturer's authorised representative in the EU is Springer Nature Customer Service Centre GmbH, Europaplatz 3, 69115 Heidelberg, Germany. If you have any concerns regarding our products, please contact ProductSafety@springernature.com

Printed and bound by CPI Group (UK) Ltd, Croydon, CR0 4YY
30/09/2026
02225514-0014